Farnsworth House

Phaidon Press Limited
Regent's Wharf
All Saints Street
London N1 9PA

Phaidon Press Inc.
180 Varick Street
New York, NY 10014

www.phaidon.com

First published 2003
Reprinted in paperback 2005
© 2003 Phaidon Press Limited

ISBN 0 7148 4558 2

A CIP catalogue record for this book is available from the British Library.

All rights reserved. No part of this publication may be reproduced, stored in a retrieval system or transmitted, in any form or by any means, electronic, mechanical, photocopying, recording or otherwise, without the written permission of Phaidon Press Limited.

Designed by Hoop Design
Printed in Hong Kong

Author's Acknowledgements

The following people gave me invaluable assistance. For this I thank them, though all mistakes of fact or interpretation are of course my own.

My text benefited from the comments of Dr Nicholas Bullock, Professor Dieter Holm, and Professor John McKean; and of Peter Carter and George Edson Danforth, both of whom were design associates in Mies's office. I received essential information from Joseph Fujikawa of Fujikawa, Johnson and Associates Inc, Chicago; Tom Blanchard at the Plano site; and Dr Wolf Tegethoff of the Zentralinstitut für Kunstgeschichte, Munich. Professor Peter Land kindly supplied a portfolio of excellent photographs without charge, and it saddens me that we could accommodate so few in the available pages.

Finally I thank Lord Palumbo and his assistant Anne Carter-Campbell for clearing away many problems; and my editors at Phaidon Press, Iona Baird and Rosie Fairhead, for their generous and expert help.

Picture credits

Tom Blanchard: figs. 49, 50; Mario Ciampi: fig. 7; Hedrich-Blessing: figs. 6, 10; John Hewitt: pp.42–54; A F Kersting: fig. 25; Peter Land: figs. 35, 36, 38, 39; p.40L; Digital images © 2002 Museum of Modern Art/Scala, Florence: figs. 4, 15; The Newberry Library, Chicago: fig. 31; Bernard Newman: fig. 32R; Franz Schulze: fig. 32L; Maritz Vandenberg: figs. 2, 3, 11–4, 16–24, 27–30, 33, 34, 40–2, 46–48. All other photographs: Peter Cook.

Farnsworth House
Ludwig Mies van der Rohe

Maritz Vandenberg
ARCHITECTURE IN DETAIL

Foreword
Lord Peter Palumbo

The Farnsworth House has this in common with Cannery Row in Monterey, California: it is a poem, a quality of light, a tone, a habit, a nostalgia, a dream. It has about it, also, an aura of high romance. The die for the romance was cast from the moment Mies van der Rohe decided to site the house next to the great black sugar maple – one of the most venerable in the county – that stands immediately to the south, within a few yards of the bank of the Fox River. The rhythms created by the juxtaposition of the natural elements and the man-made object can be seen at a glance – tree bending over house in a gesture of caress, a never-ending love affair – and felt – when the leaves of the tree brush the panes of glass on the southern elevation. In summer, the dense foliage of the sugar maple shields the house from the torrid heat and ensures its privacy from the river.

With its glass walls suspended on steel piloti almost two metres above the flood plain of the meadow, life inside the house is very much a balance with nature, and an extension of nature. A change in the season or an alteration of the landscape creates a marked change in the mood inside the house. With an electric storm of Wagnerian proportions illuminating the night sky and shaking the foundations of the house to their very core, it is possible to remain quite dry! When, with the melting of the snows in spring, the Fox River becomes a roaring torrent that bursts its banks, the house assumes the character of a house-boat, the water level sometimes rising perilously close to the front door. On such occasions, the approach to the house is by canoe, which is tied up to the steps of the upper terrace.

The overriding quality of the Farnsworth House is one of serenity. It is a very quiet house. I think this derives from the ordered logic and clarity of the whole, from the way in which the house has been lovingly crafted, and from the sensitive juxtaposition of fine materials. Anxiety, stress or sheer fatigue drop away almost overnight, and problems that had seemed insoluble assume minor proportions after the 'therapy' exerted by the house has washed over them for a few hours.

The start of the day is very important to me. At Farnsworth, the dawn can be seen or sensed from the only bed in the house, which is placed in the northeast corner. The east elevation of the house tends to be a bit poker-faced – the dawn greets the house more than the house welcomes the dawn. Shortly after sunrise the early morning light, filtering through the branches of the linden tree, first dapples and then etches the silhouette of the leaves in sharp relief upon the curtain. It is a scene no Japanese print could capture to greater effect.

People ask me how practical Farnsworth is to live in. As a home for a single person, it performs extremely well. It was never intended for anything else. The size of its single room, 55 ft by 28 ft, is a guarantee of its limitations. On the other hand, for short periods of time it is possible to sleep three people in comfort and privacy. This is a measure of the flexibility of the space, and indeed it would be odd if this were not so, for flexibility is a hallmark of Mies's work.

I believe that houses and structures are not simply inanimate objects, but have a 'soul' of their own, and the Farnsworth House is no exception. Before owning the house I had always imagined that steel and glass could not possess this quality – unlike brick, for example, which is a softer, more porous material that seems to absorb as well as emanate a particular atmosphere. But steel and glass are equally responsive to the mood of the moment. The Farnsworth House is equable by inclination and nature. It never frowns. It is sometimes sad, but rarely forlorn. Most often it smiles and chuckles, especially when it is host to children's laughter and shouts of delight. It seems to eschew pretension and to welcome informality.

Living in the house I have gradually become aware of a very special phenomenon: the man-made environment and the natural environment are here permitted to respond to, and to interact with, each other. While this may deviate from the dogma of Rousseau or the writings of Thoreau, the effect is essentially the same: that of being at one with Nature, in its broadest sense, and with oneself.

If the start of the day is important, so is the finish. That tone and quality of light shared with Cannery Row is seldom more evident than at dusk, with its graduations of yellow, green, pink and purple. At such times, one can see forever and with astonishing clarity. Sitting outside on the upper deck one feels like the lotus flower that floats in the water and never gets wet. In November, a harvest moon rises slowly behind the tree-line, as if giving a seal of approval to the day that has just gone by. Later on, in January, when the winter snows have begun to fall and the landscape is transformed, cars sweep silently past the property along frozen roads, and the magical stillness of the countryside is broken only by the plangent barking of a dog, perhaps three miles distant.

In a low-lying meadow beside the Fox River at Plano, Illinois, stands a serene pavilion of glass, steel and travertine.

When built it was unlike any known house, and a description written by the American critic Arthur Drexler soon after its completion in 1951 captures its essence: 'The Farnsworth House consists of three horizontal planes: a terrace, a floor, and a roof. Welded to the leading edge of each plane are steel columns which keep them all suspended in mid-air. Because they do not rest *on* the columns, but merely touch them in passing, these horizontal elements seem to be held to their supports by magnetism. Floor and roof appear as opaque planes defining the top and bottom of a volume whose sides are simply large panels of glass. The Farnsworth House is, indeed, a quantity of air caught between a floor and a roof.'[1]

In spring the pavilion stands on a carpet of daffodils, in summer upon a green meadow, in autumn amid the glow of golden foliage; and when the adjacent river overflows the house resembles a boat floating on the great expanse of water. It is in effect a raised stage from which an entranced viewer may not merely observe ever-changing nature, but almost experience the sensation of being within it.

It is Mies van der Rohe's last realized house, built to provide a cultivated and well-to-do urbanite with a quiet retreat where she could enjoy nature and recover from the cares of work.

The rural escape for busy city-dwellers has a long history, either as country villa[2] or, more modestly, as the simple shooting or fishing lodge.[3] But while its function was fairly well established in architectural tradition, the form and appearance of

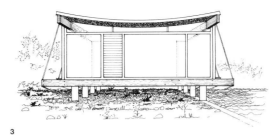

1 The Farnsworth House: a pavilion in a meadow
2 Gropius and Breuer's Chamberlain House (1940) and
3 Rudolph and Twitchell's Healy Guest House (1948–50), both cabins-on-stilts designed at roughly the same time as the Farnsworth House
4 Mies's first built house, the Riehl House of 1907
Two contrasting examples of Miesian design in the 1920s:
5 The Hermann Lange House of 1927–30, which is solid and block-like
6 The Barcelona Pavilion of 1928–9, which is transparent and pavilion-like

Farnsworth House went to the extremes of modernism, neatly inverting (as we shall see) most of the architectural devices developed over the past 2,500 years.

In view of its status as an architectural landmark we should try to locate this luculent design in two contexts – one personal (the Farnsworth House as the culmination of the architect's 40-year sequence of continually-evolving house designs) and the other much wider (the Farnsworth House as an ultimate icon of that strand of European modernism that became known as the International Style) – before going on to more practical matters such as why the house was built, how it was built, and how it has performed.

A consummation of Miesian design

At first sight Mies's first and last built houses, the Riehl House of 1907 and the Farnsworth House of 40 years later, could hardly be more different. Beneath the contrasting appearances, though, there is a recognizable continuity of design approach. From first to last there shines through Mies's work a dignified serenity, a concern for regularity and orderliness, and a precision of detailing that are just as important as the obvious differences seen in successive stages of his work.

These differences were not capricious but reflect a continuous and sustained effort – particularly after about 1920 – to eliminate what the earnest Mies saw as inessentials and to distil his buildings to some kind of irreducible architectonic essence of the age.[4]

While it is always a mistake to impose an unduly neat 'line of development' on the complex, uncertain and partly accidental career of any designer, as though each successive work represented a calculated step towards a clearly foreseen goal, hindsight does allow us to divide Mies's development into three recognizable phases. The first was pre-1919, when his designs were invariably solid, regular and soberly traditional. The

second covered the years 1919–38, when he began to experiment (though only in some of his designs) with such entrancing novelties as irregular plans, interiors designed as continuous flowing fields rather than separate rooms, extreme horizontal transparency, and floating floor and roof planes. The third was post-1938, when he returned to the classicism and sobriety of his earlier years, but expressed now in steel-framed

buildings rather than solid masonry, and incorporating the transparency and (in some of the pavilions) emphatic horizontality developed in his avant-garde projects of the 1920s.

The first of these formative periods had its roots in Mies's youth in Aachen where, the son of a master mason, he came to love the town's historic buildings. He later recalled that 'few of them were important buildings. They were mostly very simple, but very clear. I was impressed by the strength of these buildings because they did not belong to any epoch. They had been there for over a thousand years and were still impressive, and nothing could change that. All the great styles passed, but they were still there ... as good as on the day they were built.'[5]

This early affinity with sober clarity was confirmed in 1907 when he visited Italy and was deeply impressed by his first sight of Roman aqueducts, the heroic ruins of the Basilica of Constantine, and in particular the bold stonework facade of the Palazzo Pitti with its cleanly-cut window openings, of which he said: 'You see with how few means you can make architecture – and what architecture!'[6]

And it crystallized into coherent principle when in 1912, on a visit to the Netherlands, Mies encountered the work of Hendrik Petrus Berlage. He was particularly struck by Berlage's Amsterdam Stock Exchange (1903), an outstanding example of the 'monolothic' way of building – that is to say one in which the materials of construction are nakedly displayed (like the marble components of Greek temples), in contradiction to the 'layered' approach where basic materials are covered by more sophisticated claddings (like the walls of Roman architecture). The Stock Exchange walls are of unplastered brickwork inside and out, and the roof trusses completely exposed, so that there is no distinction between what is structure and what is finish, or between what is structure and what is architecture.[7] Mies later recollected that it was at that point 'that the idea of a clear construction came to me as one of the fundamentals we should accept.'[8] What especially appealed to him was Berlage's 'careful construction that was honest down to the bone', forming the basis, as Mies saw it, of 'a spiritual attitude [that] had nothing to do with classicism, nothing to do with historic styles.'[9]

Between these mutually reinforcing experiences in Aachen, Italy and Amsterdam there was a somewhat different influence – that of the German neo-classicist Karl Friedrich Schinkel, whose works Mies came to know while working in the Berlin studio of Peter Behrens between 1908 and 1912.[10] Mies did not particularly admire Schinkel's early work, which to him represented the end of a past era, but he considered that the Bauakademie of 1831–5 'introduced a new epoch'. The lessons he absorbed from Schinkel were concerned less with honest construction (though the facades of the Kaufhaus project of 1827 and the later Bauakademie did reflect their underlying structures with notable clarity) than with architectonic composition. His compositional borrowings from Schinkel included a tendency to place buildings on raised platforms to create a sense of noble repose; a stern sobriety of architectural form; highly regular spacing and careful proportioning of facade elements; and an exceptional clarity of articulation, with the separate elements of the building clearly differentiated.[11]

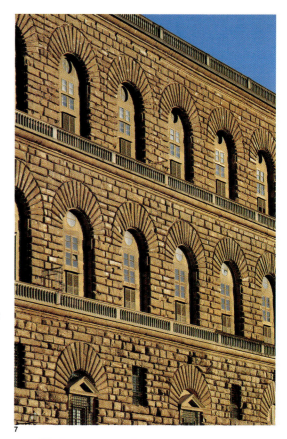

Seminal influences on Mies:
7 The bold, sharply-incised stone facade of the Palazzo Pitti in Florence, 1435
8 The rude honesty of Berlage: Amsterdam Stock Exchange, 1903
9 The compositional discipline of Schinkel: the Altes Museum in Berlin, 1822–8

Here, then, were two complementary influences that would preoccupy Mies for the rest of his life – a Berlage-like affinity with 'honesty' that led him to theorize that building form should be determined by the structural problem being solved, and the materials employed, and not by abstract rules of composition;[12] counter-balanced by a Schinkelesque love of classical form that led him in the converse direction, yearning to develop architectural forms of abstracted perfection. He was aware of the conflict, saying in 1966: 'After Berlage I had to fight with myself to get away from the classicism of Schinkel'[13] – a battle he seems largely to have lost, with the compositional sophistication of Schinkel generally prevailing over the rude honesty of Berlage.[14]

Had his development stopped at that point, Mies might have spent the rest of his career as a consummate designer of somewhat blocky buildings characterized by clarity, regularity and discipline (derived from Schinkel); making increasing use of exposed brickwork (inspired by Berlage); and showing also the powerful forms and glassiness of Peter Behrens[15] and the open interiors, powerful outward thrust and emphatic horizontality of Frank Lloyd Wright.[16]

It took years of digestion before 'inputs' became 'outputs' with the gradually-developing Mies; and while some of the above characteristics are indeed visible in the severe monumentality of the Bismarck Memorial (1910) and Kroller House (1912) projects, others were only to appear much later. One thinks for instance of the fluid interior and outward-thrusting composition of the Brick Country House project (1923–4), and of the cubic forms and immaculately-detailed brickwork of the Wolf (1925–7), Esters (1927–30) and Lange (1927–30) houses. These designs are especially notable for their Berlage-like use of weighty, unplastered brickwork walls at a time when European modernism strove mostly for a smooth, white, lightweight appearance.

After returning from military service in January 1919, Mies underwent an astonishing transformation, and began a distinct second developmental phase. Berlin was then in a ferment of avant-garde activity, both political and artistic; Mies was willingly caught up in these movements,[17] and in 1921 he began to produce a sequence of projects that bore little resemblance to anything he (or indeed anyone else) had done before. These designs, manifesto-like in their vivid clarity, helped to change the face of twentieth-century architecture, and their influence would be unmistakably visible in the later Farnsworth House.

His experiments from 1919–38 involved progressive transformations of the kind of *space* that is shaped by architecture, and of the kind of *structure* that helps do the shaping.

The Glass Skyscraper project of 1922 (figure 10), with its open interiors and transparent envelope and its clear distinction between structure (slim columns and hovering slabs) and claddings (a diaphonous skin), presents a vivid illustration of Mies's spatial and structural ideas.[18] But this project is an office building, and the specific antecedents of the Farnsworth House are more appropriately traced in his house designs, so it is to those that we must turn.

Looking then at Mies's development in the specific context of house design, his spatial ideas may be summarized as follows. First he started to dissolve the interior subdivisions of the dwelling, moving away from the box-like rooms of traditional western architecture towards more open interiors – the latter probably showing the intertwined influences of Frank Lloyd Wright, the Japanese house[19] and the De Stijl movement.[20] The first hints of this progressive opening-up and thinning-out of the interior appear in the unrealized Brick Country House project. Its Berlage-like brick walls, while as solidly-built and densely-packed as those of the past, are loosely arranged to suggest rather than enclose a series of doorless spaces that substituted for rooms.[21] The idea is partly realized in the 1928–30 Tugendhat House, whose main floor is opened up to become a single space within which dining, living and study areas are lightly suggested by screens of maccassar ebony, onyx and translucent glass. The final step, via a series of unbuilt projects,[22] is the Farnsworth House which has no full-height internal subdivisions except for a service core enclosing separate bathrooms and a utility room.

Parallel to the above process Mies also started to dissolve the boundary between inside and outside. The plan of the unbuilt Brick Country House, while clearly influenced by Frank Lloyd Wright,[23] opens out into the site in a way unprecedented in western architecture. The Glass Room at the Werkbund Exhibition of 1927 uses glass walls to reduce the distinction between inside and outside. And finally came the 1928–9 Barcelona Pavilion, an assembly of free-standing partitions under a floating roof in which it is quite impossible to say at

10

11

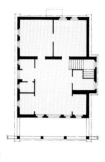

12

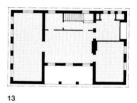

13

what point 'inside' becomes 'outside'. Though in many ways hauntingly house-like (hence its inclusion in this genealogy) this was a non-inhabited pavilion with no need for enclosing walls, thus allowing the architect to take liberties that would be impossible in a true dwelling.[24] But once conceived, the idea kept re-emerging in subsequent house designs (see figures 19–22) and again reaches a climax in the glass-walled Farnsworth House.

The spatial opening-up of the house described above was interconnected with the parallel development of Mies's structural ideas from the early 1920s to the early 1940s.

Mies's long-standing love of clearly-displayed structure found a natural means of expression in the steel-framed apartment and office buildings of Chicago, where he settled in 1938,[25] and where his third period of development as suggested on p.7 may be said to have begun. The outcome of his engagement with the Chicago steel frame, seen to perfection in the Farnsworth House, was what he himself referred to as 'skin and bones' design – a thin external skin (preferably glass) fitted to a skeletal frame (preferably steel) of the utmost clarity and elegance, with maximum differentiation between load-bearing frame and non-load-bearing skin.[26]

In this last period his work underwent a marked change of temper. Seemingly sated with the irregular plans and free-floating planes of the avant-garde experiments of the 1920s, Mies rather surprisingly reverted after about 1938 to the sober classicism of his early architecture, shown now in buildings with steel frames rather than stone. All that survives from the 1920s projects is a very modern transparency and (in some of his pavilions) a use of floating planes.

Two points must be added to the above analysis. While the essentially aesthetic experiments with space and structure outlined above are the central story of Mies's second and third phases of evolution as a designer, it would be an over-simplification to see the form and appearance of the Farnsworth House as the outcome only of aesthetic concerns.

There were also social issues at work. Nineteenth-century European cities were haunted by disease, particularly tuberculosis; and Mies shared a widespread early-twentieth-century yearning for a new way of living that would be simpler, cleaner and healthier than before. The theme of wholesome living in airy, sunny rooms (in contrast with the stuffy, dusty and over-furnished buildings of nineteenth-century architecture) is seen in countless early twentieth-century writings, architectural

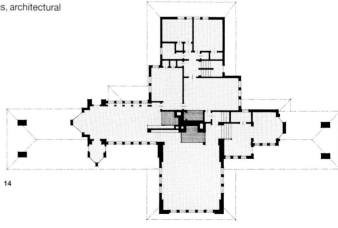

14

10 Mies's Glass Skyscraper project of 1922: a stack of horizontal planes sheathed in glass
11 Plan of a traditional twentieth-century German house (anonymous). For easy comparison, figures 12–15, 17–25 and 28–9 are all reproduced to a common scale of approximately 1:500 (in some instances the exact scale is not known)
12 Plan of Mies's Riehl House, 1907
13 Plan of Mies's Perls house, 1910–11
14 In contrast with the above, Frank Lloyd Wright's relatively open, outward-thrusting Ward W Willits Residence plan, designed in 1901 and first published in Germany (along with figure 10 and many others) in 1910–11
15 Theo van Doesburg's painting *Rhythm of a Russian Dance*, 1918
16 Mies's Brick Country House, 1923 (unbuilt)

and other, and led naturally to the clinically white, glassy and sparsely furnished buildings of Mies and his contemporaries.

And there was, secondly, a spiritual aspect. Throughout his life the apparently technology-driven Mies van der Rohe was actually an earnest searcher after the deeper meanings behind everyday existence.[27] Some time between 1924 and 1927 he moved to the view that 'building art is always the spatial expression of spiritual decisions' and began to gravitate away from the rather mechanistic functionalists of the *Neue Sachlichkeit* ('new objectivity') movement.[28] He had for many years been pondering the writings of Catholic philosophers such as St Thomas Aquinas, and now discovered a new book by Siegfried Ebeling titled *Der Raum als Membran*. This was a mystical tract which treated the building as an enclosing membrane forming a space for concentration and mystic celebration.[29] It is clear from the underlinings in Mies's personal copy that he took Ebeling's arguments seriously.

Though this period of spirituality seems to have faded somewhat after his Barcelona Pavilion, and he gradually returned to drier and more objective design attitudes as noted above, the dignified serenity of pavilions such as the Farnsworth House and the New National Gallery in Berlin (1962–8) bear witness to Mies's abiding preoccupation with the creation of orderly, noble and indeed quasi-spiritual spaces in our turbulent world.

The outcome at Fox River of all the themes traced above – aesthetic, social and spiritual – is a tranquil weekend house of unsurpassed clarity, simplicity and elegance. Every physical element has been distilled to its irreducible essence. The

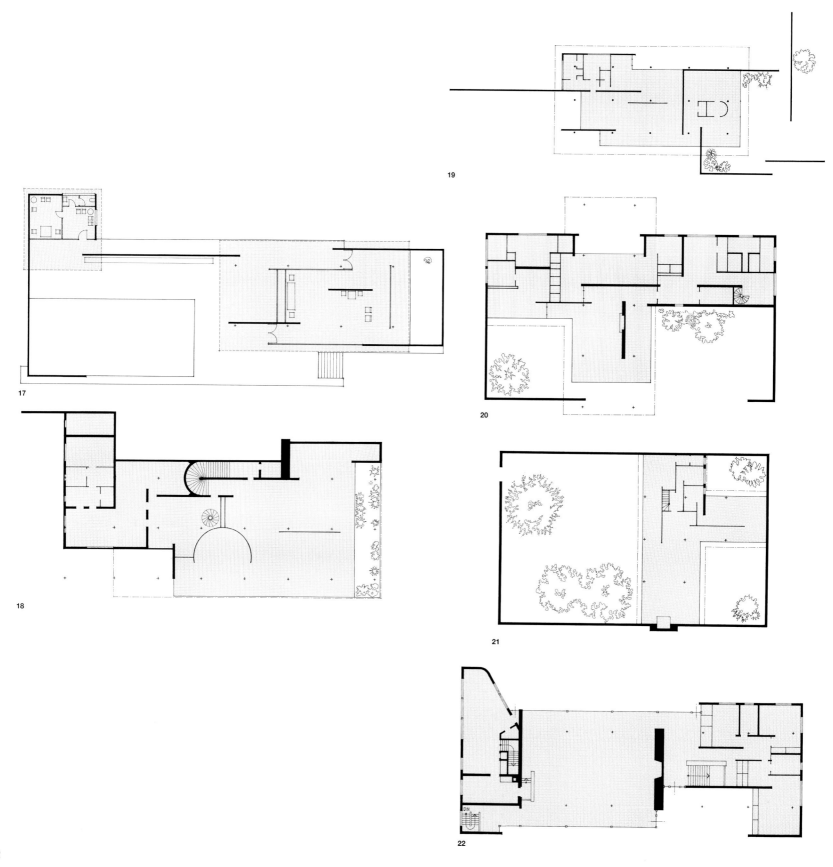

17 Mies's German Pavilion at Barcelona Exposition, 1928–9
18 The main (living-area) floor of his Tugendhat House, 1928–30
19 Mies's House for a Childless Couple. Exhibit at the Berlin Building Exposition, 1931
20 Hubbe House, 1935 (unbuilt)
21 Three-court courtyard house, 1930s (unbuilt)
22 Resor House, 1938 (unbuilt)
23 Early sketch of the 50 × 50 ft house, showing a service core surrounded by loosely-arranged partitions within a glass-walled enclosure
24 Plan of the 50 × 50 ft house, 1950–1 (unbuilt)
25 A characteristic late nineteenth-century room: the Linley Sambourne House, London, 1890s
26 The living area of the Farnsworth House

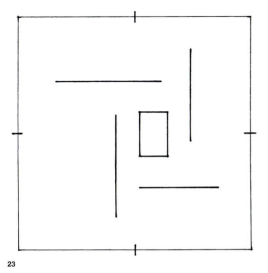

interior is unprecedentedly transparent to the surrounding site, and also unprecedentedly uncluttered in itself. All the paraphernalia of traditional architecture and traditional living – rooms, walls, doors, interior trim, loose furniture, pictures on walls, even personal possessions – have been virtually abolished in a puritanical vision of simplified, transcendental existence. Mies had finally achieved a goal towards which he had been feeling his way for three decades.[30]

An icon of modernism
Though welcomed by the American architectural establishment – a leading journal commented that the house was 'a concentration of pure beauty' and had 'no equal in perfection of workmanship [and] precision of detail'[31] – the Farnsworth House was nevertheless distinctly un-American, a late product of the European-born International Style[32] which filtered into America in about 1932 but never took root there except in the field of office design.[33]

In house design the dominant American architects of the 1940s were regionalists and vernacularists who, while influenced by the International Style, had quickly started to open up its closed forms, adapt them to regional climates, enrich its white surfaces with natural and vernacular materials, and generally accommodate a stiff, chilly style to the informality and comfortable living of popular American culture.[34] Behind all these developments loomed of course the rapidly reviving influence of Frank Lloyd Wright, who had always detested the whiteness and thinness of the International Style and its lack of rootedness in site, landscape, or in American culture.[35]

Mies stood aside from all these developments. Though now living in America, and basing virtually all his post-1938 designs on the Chicago steel frame, he remained resolutely European in his determination to intellectualize this essentially workaday and often rough form of construction, continually trying to transmute and refine industrial steel to (in the case of the Farnsworth House) something approaching a modern equivalent of Greek marble.[36]

To understand the Farnsworth House as an ultimate icon of the International Style one may briefly note some of the characteristics of this movement, and in particular its practitioners' determination to invert almost every characteristic of the architecture of the past 2,500 years, striving wherever possible (like rebellious teenagers yearning to shock their elders) to do the exact opposite.

Thus, where traditional buildings were characterized (and usually dominated) by pitched roofs, modernists decreed that roofs must be flat. Where traditional buildings were vertically composed and had predominantly vertical windows, modernists insisted on horizontally composed buildings with a notable use of horizontal strip windows. Where traditional buildings were essentially heavy-looking, solid and opaque, those of the modernist were light, and preferably transparent. Where traditional buildings rested firmly on the earth, modern ones must be raised on stilts or exploit the cantilever to appear to float above the earth. Where traditional buildings were recognisably site-built, modern ones must resemble factory

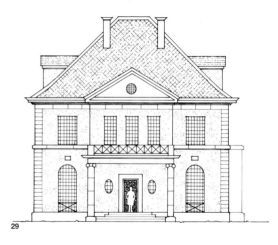
29

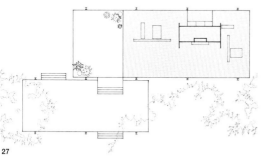
27

28

products – even if the effect had to be faked, as it usually was. Where traditional buildings were ornamented, modern buildings must be bare. Where traditional houses had rooms, modern ones must be open-plan. Where traditional rooms were thickly carpeted and curtained, and densely filled with furniture and bric-a-brac, modern ones must have hard, clean surfaces and be virtually devoid of furniture and possessions.

And so on. Though there were important continuities between classicism and modernism,[37] stylistic inversions such as those above (and others which interested readers may trace for themselves) dominated the mostly white, glassy, flat-surfaced, sparsely-furnished buildings selected for publication in 1932 in *The International Style*, five of them by Mies van der Rohe.[38] In the Farnsworth House these characteristics are taken so far, and distilled into a composition of such elegance and single-minded clarity, that it can stand as a late icon of what the International Style of the late 1920s and early 1930s had been 'trying to be'.

Client, site and brief

In late 1945 Mies van der Rohe, then aged 59 and still relatively unknown in America,[39] met (probably at a dinner party) an intelligent and art-conscious 42-year-old Chicago medical specialist called Edith Farnsworth.[40] She mentioned in conversation that she owned a riverside site on the Fox River, about 60 miles west of Chicago, and was thinking of building there a weekend retreat. She wondered aloud whether his office might be interested. He was, and after several excursions to the site with Edith Farnsworth he was given the commission.

It was, for Mies, an ideal challenge. A cabin for weekend use by a single person was the kind of programme to which he best responded. Rather like the Barcelona Pavilion of 1928–9[41] the Farnsworth House was a project in which the tiresome realities of everyday life (the need for privacy, the accumulation of possessions, the daily litter and clutter) could be disregarded in a single-minded quest for transcendental elegance.

The site was a narrow seven-acre strip of deciduous woodland beside the Fox River. Its southern boundary was formed by the river-bank and a thin line of trees; the northern boundary by a gentle grassy rise and a thicker grove of trees, along which ran a minor public road giving access to the site. The eastern boundary was also formed by a grove of trees; and the western boundary by Fox River Drive, the main road to Plano. Between these features lay a grassy meadow, idyllically isolated except for the (then) lightly-used road to the west.

Initial progress was rapid. Mies started designing within a year, and a model closely resembling the final design was exhibited at the Museum of Modern Art in New York in 1947. He was ready to proceed but Dr Farnsworth had to wait for an inheritance before authorizing a start on site. Construction finally began in September 1949, and the house was completed in 1951.

The lawsuit

By then, unfortunately, the initially sympathetic relationship between architect and client had turned sour. Everyone who

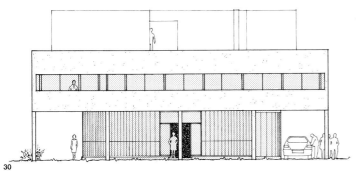

27, 28 Preliminary and final plans of the Farnsworth House
29 An early twentieth-century villa in Aachen (anonymous)
30 Le Corbusier's Villa Savoye, 1928–9

knew them agrees that this was at least partly due to a failed romance between Mies van der Rohe and Edith Farnsworth. At the start of the project they worked closely together, had picnics on the river bank, and Dr Farnsworth was breathlessly excited by both the man and the emerging design. Recalling the evening she first discussed the house with Mies she later said that 'the effect was tremendous, like a storm, a flood, or an Act of God.'[42] And in June 1946, a few months after that revelatory evening, she sent Mies a handwritten letter:

'Dear Mies
It is impossible to pay in money for what is made by heart and soul! Such work one can only recognize and cherish – with love and respect. But the concrete world affects us both and I must recognize that also and see that it is dealt with in some decent fashion.
So, dear Mies, I am enclosing a cheque for one thousand [dollars] on account, with full awareness of its inadequacy.
Faithfully yours
Edith'

The romance went wrong, unkind remarks began to be made on both sides,[43] and in 1953 Mies sued Dr Farnsworth for unpaid fees of $28,173. She countersued for $33,872, alleging a large cost over-run on the original budget, a leaking roof and excessive condensation on the glass walls.[44]

After a court hearing that must have been excruciatingly painful for both sides, Mies van der Rohe and Edith Farnsworth in mid-1953 agreed a $14,000 settlement in Mies's favour.

The battle continued outside the courtroom. Many architects and critics had been overwhelmed by the clarity, polish and precision of the design but the April 1953 issue of the more populist (and in many respects more realistic) *House Beautiful* attacked the house itself, the International Style of which it is an exemplar, and the Bauhaus which was the seedbed of this kind of design. The author, Elizabeth Gordon, accused the architecture of being 'cold' and 'barren'; the furniture 'sterile', 'thin' and 'uncomfortable'; Mies's design as an attack on traditional American values.[45]

Frank Lloyd Wright, who in the 1930s and early 1940s had admired Mies's work and regarded him as a friend,[46] joined in: 'The International Style ... is totalitarianism. These Bauhaus architects ran from political totalitarianism in Germany to what is now made by specious promotion to seem their own totalitarianism in art here in America ...'[47]

Edith Farnsworth added her own angry comments, then and later, about the general impossibility of living in her exquisite glass pavilion. She complained that 'Mies talks about his "free space", but the space is very fixed. I can't even put a clothes hanger in my house without considering how it affects everything from the outside'; and that 'I thought you could animate a pre-determined, classic form like this with your own presence. I wanted to do something meaningful and all I got was this glib, false sophistication.'[48] It may of course be that her views were coloured by the extremity of her bitterness towards Mies.[49] As Professor Dieter Holm suggested to me in conversation, had she envisaged her exquisite pavilion as a kind of Japanese tea house in which she and her friend and mentor would conduct exalted discussions about life and art;[50] and were her subsequent attacks an expression of rage at the man who had let her down, rather than a comment on the house?

It seems likely. Despite her criticisms Edith Farnsworth continued to use the house until 1971, though treating it with scant respect. Adrian Gale saw it in 1958 and found 'a sophisticated camp site rather than a weekend dreamhouse'. When its subsequent purchaser Peter Palumbo visited Dr Farnsworth in 1971 he was depressed to see an approach path of crazy paving; the western terrace enclosed by mosquito screens so that one entered the glass pavilion via a wire mesh door; the once-beautiful primavera panels veneered to a blackish, reddish colour; the floor space unpleasantly blocked by mostly nondescript furniture; and the sink piled high with dishes which had not been washed for several days.

A year later the Farnsworth House was sold, and entered upon a happier phase of existence, as will be related in the Postscript on p.24.

Planning

Before turning to the planning of the Farnsworth House itself, that of its immediate predecessors must be considered. The emphatic horizontal planes, glass-walled transparency and open interiors which Mies had been perfecting since 1921 had come together in a sublime synthesis in the Barcelona Pavilion.[51] Having crystallized his ideas in that essentially ceremonial and functionless building, where such experiments in abstraction could be carried out relatively freely, Mies began

31

also to incorporate them in a sequence of house designs.

The first of these was a grand residence for Fritz and Grete Tugendhat, which Mies was actually in the process of designing when he was commissioned to undertake the Barcelona Pavilion. The Tugendhats were enlightened newly-weds who wanted a modern house with generous spaces and clear, simple forms; and who were aware of Mies's work. They arranged a meeting in 1928 – and like many previous clients (and his future client Dr Edith Farnsworth) were bowled over by his massive presence and air of calm self-assurance. As Mrs Tugendhat said later: 'From the first moment it was certain that he was our man ... We knew we were in the same room with an artist.' That was a common reaction among Mies's clients.[52]

Architect-client relations were not quite as smooth as here implied, but the project went ahead. The Tugendhat House was completed in 1930 and represented a decisive step away from the solid 'block' houses Mies had been building only two years earlier (the Esters and Lange houses of 1927–30), and towards the transparent 'pavilion' houses he would be designing in the future. The living room was extensive and tranquil, enclosed by glass walls so transparent that the outer landscape and sky seemed almost to form the room boundaries. The room was subtly zoned into conversation, dining, study and library areas by only two or three free-standing partitions and a few precisely-placed pieces of furniture. It was virtually empty except for these artwork-like items of furniture, and there was no allowance for pictures on the walls.

In another pre-figuration of the Farnsworth House the colours were predominantly neutral and unassertive. The floor was covered in creamy, off-white linoleum. There was a black silk curtain before the glass wall by the winter garden; a silvery-grey silk curtain before the main glass wall; the library could be closed off by a white velvet curtain; and a black velvet curtain ran between the onyx wall and the winter garden. This neutral backdrop heightened the dramatic effect of a few carefully-devised focal points – the rich black-and-brown ebony curved partition; the tawny-gold onyx flat partition; the emerald-green leather, ruby-red velvet, and white vellum furniture claddings; and the lush green jungle of plants filling the winter garden.

After many experimental drawing-board projects Mies was beginning to realize in built form that 'puritanical vision of simplified, transcendental existence' referred to on p.13.

This vision had its negative side, and along with the plaudits the Tugendhat House began to attract comments of a kind that would recur with the Farnsworth House. Gropius called it a 'Sunday house', questioning its suitability for everyday living, and a critic asked unkindly, 'Can one live in House Tugendhat?' – a question the Tugendhats answered with an impassioned 'yes'.[53]

There followed the House for a Childless Couple at the Berlin Fair (1931), which distinctly recalls the Barcelona Pavilion; and then a series of unbuilt Courtyard House designs (1931–8) in which Mies tested on confined urban sites the concept of open-plan interiors, sheltering beneath horizontal roof planes and looking out on to gardens via glass walls. One-, two- or three-court houses were planned, the entire site in each case being surrounded by a brick wall. Within the privacy of these enclosures each individual house faced its courtyard via a thin-framed, ceiling-height glass wall. Interiors consisted of few rooms and large areas of continuous, fluid space very reminiscent of the Brick Country House project; and roofs were lightly supported on the external walls plus four to eight slender columns, leaving the internal partitions free of all load-bearing function. Space flowed freely through the interiors and out into the courtyards. Each walled enclosure was effectively one large 'room', part of which was indoors and part outdoors – an intermediate stage to the Farnsworth House where the entire surrounding meadow would become an extension of the glass-walled interior.

In 1937–8, as Mies was in the process of emigrating to Chicago, came the immediate forerunner of the Farnsworth House. This was a design (alas, unbuilt) for a summer residence for Mr and Mrs Stanley Resor bridging a small river in Wyoming.[54] Very appropriately for his first American building, the central 'bridge' section of the house was a long steel-framed box. This was raised slightly clear of the site, formed a glass-walled living area, and had no internal divisions except for furniture and a fireplace.

Interestingly, Mies's previous intimate incorporation of houses into their landscapes begins here to give way to a distinct separation between the man-made object and nature.[55] In the past, the interior spaces (the wings of the house) and exterior spaces (the gardens and courtyards) were intimately interlocked in projects as late as the Esters and Lange houses. Here, while the ends of the Resor House – whose foundations

32

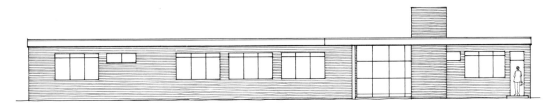

31 Dr Edith Farnsworth in early and later life
32 Mies van der Rohe in 1912 (left) and mid-1950s
33 Draft elevation of Mies's unbuilt Ulrich Lange House, 1935
34 Street elevation of his unbuilt House with Three Courtyards, 1930s

were inherited by Mies from an earlier design for that site – are firmly rooted to the site, the bridge-like central section parts company with the landscape, hovering aloofly above an untouched site. By a quirk of fate the site problem which generated this elevated geometry – regular floodwaters – would recur with his next house.

In 1946, on Dr Farnsworth's plot beside the Fox River, Mies could finally bring all these gradually-evolved ideas to their ultimate conclusion.

His most fundamental decision involved the relationship between the building and the landscape – a relationship that aimed at bringing nature, the house and human beings together into 'a higher unity', as he put it.

The house stands about 1.6 metres (just over 5 ft) above the surrounding meadow, leaving the site completely undisturbed and giving its occupants a magnificent belvedere from which to contemplate the surrounding woodland. The practical reason for the raised floor is that the meadow is a floodplain, but Mies has characteristically managed to transmute a technical solution to an aesthetic masterstroke. Being elevated, the house is detached from disorderly reality and becomes an exalted place for contemplation – safe, serene and perfect in all its smooth, machine-made details.

The basic arrangement of the Farnsworth House was quickly settled, but the precise layout went through the usual painstaking process of Miesian fine-tuning (his most characteristic injunction to students and design assistants was, it is said, to 'work on it some more'). Literally hundreds of preliminary drawings were produced, and these show Mies trying out several alternative positions for the access stairs, the central core and other minor elements before achieving finality.[56] Note, for instance, on figure 27, the two glass screens separating the kitchen space from the rest of the house – Mies's last half-hearted attempt at traditional boxed-in rooms before going for a completely undivided living area.[57]

Another abandoned idea was the enclosure of the western terrace by insect-proof screening. The screens were shown on the model exhibited at the Museum of Modern Art in 1947, but Mies never liked these transparency-destroying elements and the house was built without them. (In fact practicality would soon triumph over aesthetics, and the idea had to be resurrected after Dr Farnsworth moved into the house, owing to the tormenting clouds of mosquitoes rising from the riverside meadow every summer. Stainless steel screens were therefore designed and installed at her request in 1951. The work was done under Mies's supervision by his design assistant William Dunlap, client/architect relations by then being frosty.[58] The screens were removed two decades later by the new owner Peter Palumbo, and the mosquito-breeding meadow mown down to a more lawn-like surface as will be related later.)

The interior as finally realized is a single glass-enclosed space, unpartitioned except for a central service core. The latter conceals two bathrooms (one for Dr Farnsworth, one for visitors) and a utility room, and is set closer to the northern wall than to the southern. This off-centre location creates a narrow kitchen space to the north and a much larger living area to the south. The long northern side of the core consists of a single run of cabinets above a kitchen worktop, and the long southern side incorporates a low, open hearth facing the living area. The two short sides contain the entrance doors to the bathrooms.

The living area is zoned into a sleeping area on the east (thus conforming with the excellent precept, going back to Vitruvius's Sixth Book of Architecture, that bedrooms should face east so that the sleeper wakes to the glory of the morning sun), a dining area to the west, and a general sitting area between the two. The sleeping zone is served by a freestanding teak-faced cupboard.

Outside, the raised terrace to the west is a splendid place for sitting at the end of the day, watching the sunset.

Turning from internal to external planning, it seems to have been decided that allowing motor vehicles to drive right up to the pavilion (a formative design factor in another twentieth-century country villa, Le Corbusier's Villa Savoye of 1929–31) would impair the Farnsworth House's idyllic sense of seclusion. Therefore Mies's design made no provision for car access.

Dr Farnsworth did subsequently build a conventional two-car garage beside the gate on the northern boundary of the site, where she presumably parked her car and walked across the field to the house. Her visitors more commonly drove all the way to the house and parked there. The disturbing presence of garage, track and automobiles inevitably diminished the dream-like image of a small pavilion in remote woodland and, as outlined on p.25, its next owner radically replanned the site to overcome this defect.

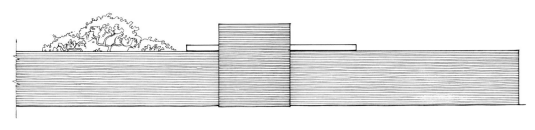

The structure

The basic structure of Farnsworth House consists of eight wide-flange steel stanchions A, to which are welded two sets of fascia channels to form a perimeter frame B at roof level, and a similar perimeter frame C at floor level – see figure 40.

Sets of steel cross-girders D and E are welded to the longitudinal channels, and pre-cast concrete planks I and N placed upon these to form the roof and floor slabs respectively. The loading imposed upon C by the floor construction is obviously greater than that imposed on B by the roof, but for the sake of visual consistency Mies has made them of equal depth – an example of the primacy of 'form' over 'function' to which he was in principle opposed,[59] but which stubbornly emerges in almost all his mature work.[60]

The steel stanchions stop short of the channel cappings, making it clear that the roof plane does not rest on the columns but merely touches them in passing, thus helping to create the impression alluded to at the start of this essay – that the horizontal elements appear to be held to their vertical supports by magnetism.

Above the roof slab is a low service module containing water tank, boiler, extract fans from the two bathrooms and a flue from the fireplace. Beneath the floor slab is a cylindrical drum housing all drainage pipes and incoming water and electrical services.

Steelwork

As the Farnsworth House is probably the most complete and refined statement of glass-and-steel architecture Mies ever produced – the ultimate crystallization of an idea, as Peter Blake has put it – it is worth examining this aspect in detail.

Mies's admiration for the structural clarity of the steel frame long predates his arrival in Chicago, and was no doubt motivated by reasons both aesthetic and practical.[61] Aesthetically the steel frame lent itself to clear structural display, and was 'honest' and free of rhetoric or historical associations – highly-prized characteristics to the future-worshipping avant-garde of the 1920s. From a practical standpoint the steel frame allowed open-plan interiors in which walls could be freely disposed,[62] and even more importantly it seemed to hold the answer to Mies's dream of traditional construction methods being replaced by industrial systems in which all the building parts could be factory-made and then rapidly assembled on-site.[63]

His move to Chicago in 1938 brought him to a city with unparalleled expertise in steel construction. Until then he had been able to use the steel frame only in a semi-concealed way;[64] but after 1937–8 the nakedly exposed rolled steel beam, uncamouflaged by covering layers of 'architecture' (except where required by fire-safety codes), would begin to form the basis of his most characteristic designs.

But whereas American builders used the steel frame with no-nonsense practicality,[65] the European Mies had different priorities. Ignoring his own arguments of fifteen years earlier that 'form is not an end in itself',[66] and that the use of materials should be determined by constructive requirements, he set about refining and intellectualizing the steel frame in what may best be described as a quest for ideal Platonic form.[67]

Thus, while the American avant-garde constructed their steel houses on the practical and economical balloon-frame principle, with slender steel members spaced fairly closely together (see for instance Richard Neutra's Lovell 'Health' House of 1927–9 and Charles Eames' Case Study House of 1949), Mies used heavy steel sections, spaced widely apart and with no visible cross-bracing to give an unprecedentedly open appearance (see especially his Farnsworth House and New National Gallery). For added character he chose for his stanchions not the commonly-used steel profiles of the time but a wide-flanged profile notable for its handsome proportions and precision of form.

Mies also departed from standard Chicago practice in his steel-jointing techniques. Flanged steel sections are popular in the construction industry partly for the ease with which they may be bolted or riveted together. The flanges are easily drilled, holes can take the form of elongated slots to accommodate slight inaccuracies, and all the basic operations are speedy and straightforward.

Mies used conventional bolted connections in the less visible parts of his structures, but in exposed positions he wished his elegant steel members to be displayed cleanly, uncluttered by bolts, rivets or plates; and here he defied normal practice by using more expensive welded joints, preferably concealed and invisible. If the weld could not be totally hidden he would have the steel sections temporarily joined by means of Nelson stud bolts and cleats, apply permanent welding, and then burn off

35, 36 'In autumn the green turns to a golden glow...'

37 'In summer the great room floats above a green meadow, its visual boundaries extending to the leafy screen of deciduous trees encircling the house, and the high sun bouncing off the travertine surface of the covered terrace...'

38, 39 'On sunny days the white steel profiles receive bright articulation and precise modelling from the sun's rays; on dull days the diffuse light will still pick out the profiles of these architectural elements...'

the holding bolts and plug the holes. The steel surfaces would then be ground smooth to give the appearance of being formed of a single continuous material without breaks or joints. Finally, to ensure a smooth and elegant appearance he had the steel sections grit-blasted to a smooth matt surface, and the entire assembly primed and given three coats of paint.

The effect of this sequence of operations in the Farnsworth House was, as Franz Schulze has commented, almost to de-industrialize the steel frame, taming the mighty product of blast furnace, rolling mill and electric arc into a silky-surfaced, seemingly jointless white substance of Platonic perfection.

Other materials

Passing on from the steel-and-glass envelope, the other materials used in the Farnsworth House are rigorously restricted to travertine (floors), wood (primavera for the core walls, teak for the wardrobe) and plaster (ceilings).

The range of colours is equally limited, the better to set off the few artworks and carefully-chosen items of furniture inside, and the framed views of nature outside – white columns and ceiling, off-white floors and curtains, and pale brown wood. Such sobriety was a long-standing Miesian characteristic. In 1958 he told the architect and critic Christian Norberg-Schulz: 'I hope to make my buildings neutral frames in which man and artworks can carry on their own lives ... Nature, too, shall have its own life. We must beware not to disrupt it with the colour of our houses and interior fittings. Yet we should attempt to bring nature, houses and human beings together into a higher unity.

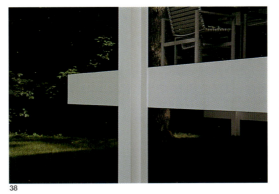

Steel frame

A Steel stanchion
B Steel channels forming perimeter frame at roof level
C Steel channels forming perimeter frame at floor level
D Steel cross-girders at roof level
E Steel cross-girders at floor level
F Intermediate mullion built up from flat steel bars

Roof construction

G Waterproof membrane on
H Foam glass insulation on
I Precast concrete planks

Floor construction

J Travertine slabs on
K Mortar bed on
L Crushed stone on
M Metal tray on
N Lightweight concrete fill on precast concrete slabs

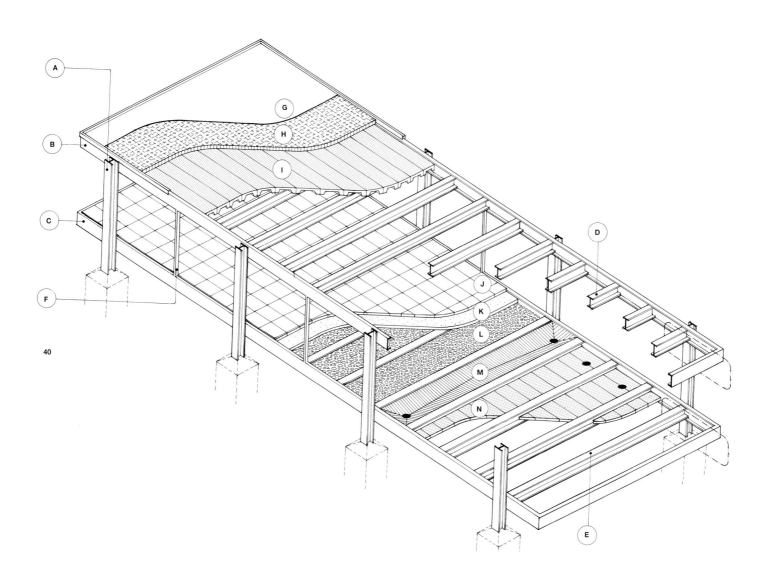

40

40 Construction of the Farnsworth House   **41** Fluidly-shaped joints in a Louis XV chair and in Mies's Barcelona chair

If you view nature through the glass walls of the Farnsworth House, it gains a more profound significance than if viewed from outside ... it becomes a part of a larger whole.'[68]

Detailing
As one would expect of Mies, the use of materials in the Farnsworth House is immaculate.[69] The American journal *Architectural Forum* commented that the Italian travertine slabs that form the floors of house and terrace were fitted to the steel frames 'with a precision equal to that of the finest incastro stonework', and that the plaster ceiling had 'the smoothness of a high-grade factory finish'.[70]

Looking at the details more closely, one discerns a typically Miesian grammar that places his classically-inspired detailing at the opposite pole to that represented by arts and crafts-influenced designers such as Greene and Greene.[71] Whereas the Greene brothers exuberantly celebrate the act of joining materials, with an abundance of highly visible fasteners intimating what goes on behind the surface, Mies hides his fixings deep within the structure so as to leave his surfaces smooth and unbroken.

The joints between components also display a characteristically Miesian grammar. Wherever two adjoining components are structurally unified, as in the case of steel members welded together, Mies expresses unification by making the meeting-point invisible – hence the process already described of grinding, polishing, priming and painting aimed at making an assembly of separate steel members look like a single, seamless casting. This approach is first seen in the X-crossing of his Barcelona Chair, whose appearance Adrian Gale has compared with those curviform eighteenth-century chairs whose legs and rails are fluidly shaped, and invisibly jointed, to convey an impression of the whole frame having been carved from a single block of wood.

But wherever two adjoining components are connected without being structurally fused, as in the case of stone slabs, timber panels or screwed (not welded) steel members, Mies takes the converse approach and emphasizes their separate identities by inserting between them a neat open groove. In the Farnsworth House such an indentation separates the plaster of the ceiling from the steel frames that hold the glass walls.

While the use of a groove between adjoining elements was not invented by him (it occurs in the work of both Schinkel and Behrens, the latter using it for instance to separate window or door frames from adjoining wall surfaces), Mies came gradually to replace most of the traditional cover strips with 'reveals' or 'flash gaps' – the respective American and British terms for the separating groove. The process may be traced as follows.

In his pre-1920 houses, from the Riehl House to the Urbig House of 1914, Mies generally used conventional interior trim to cover building joints. In his Lange House he was still using cornices, architraves, skirtings and other cover mouldings, but reduced now to simple flat strips.[72] In the Barcelona Pavilion he took the last step: there are no longer any skirtings or cornices, no column bases or capitals, and no applied trim of any kind except for glazing beads around the glass screens. Surfaces are clean and sheer, the junctions between them unconcealed.

But cover strips over the joints in a building have a function and cannot simply be abolished. Where separate components or different materials meet, the fit is inevitably imperfect, leading to an unsightly crack. The crack worsens as repeated differential movement causes the gap to widen and become ragged – a process called 'fretting' – and some form of camouflage must be devised. The traditional cover strip disguises the joint by concealment; the open groove does so by making the crack less obtrusive, an observer's eye tending to 'read' the straight-edged groove rather than the irregular crack-line meandering within it. After about 1940 this was Mies's preferred method for detailing all building joints. It is also of course an instance of the phenomenon of 'inversion' noted on p.13, the open groove being the counterform of the cover strip.

Internal environment
As regards thermal comfort, the Farnsworth House performed poorly before the implementation in the 1970s of corrective measures. In hot weather the interior could become oven-like owing to inadequate cross-ventilation and no sun-screening except for the foliage of adjacent trees. To create some cross-ventilation occupants could open the entrance doors on the west and two small hopper windows on the east, and activate an electric exhaust fan in the kitchen floor, but these measures were often inadequate. In cold weather the underfloor hot-water coils produced the pleasant heat output characteristic of such systems (partly radiant, and with temperatures at head-

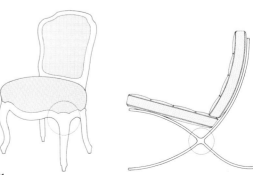

41

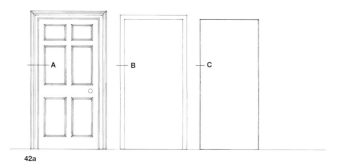

42a

level not much higher than at floor-level), but insufficient in mid-winter. Underfloor systems also have a long warming-up period that is ill-suited to an intermittently occupied house. To increase the supply of heat, and give quicker warming, hot air could be blown into the living area from a small furnace in the utility room. There was also a somewhat ineffective fireplace set into the south face of the central core, facing the living area, which it is said to have covered with a layer of ash.

The worst cold-weather failing was the amount of condensation streaming down the chilled glass panes and collecting on the floor – one of Dr Edith Farnsworth's complaints in the 1953 court case as described on p.15. This was an elementary design fault whose consequences Mies must have foreseen and could have avoided, but presumably chose to ignore so as not to destroy the beautiful simplicity of his glass-and-steel facades.[73]

As regards electric lighting, the living and sleeping areas are illuminated by uplighting reflected off the ceiling, augmented by freestanding chrome lamps. The quality of the lighting thus produced is entirely to the present owner's satisfaction.

Rainwater drainage
Efficient rainwater disposal requires sloping surfaces, a characteristic that is somewhat at odds with the perfect horizontals of Mies's design, but the problem is neatly solved in the Farnsworth House. Behind its level fascia the roof surface slopes down to a single drainage pipe directly above the utility room stack. The steel fascia and its capping stand sufficiently high above the roof surface to conceal the sloping roof from all surrounding sight-lines, and to prevent water spilling over the edge and staining the white paint.

The travertine-paved terrace has a perfectly level upper surface and yet remains dry. This has been achieved by laying the slabs on gravel beds contained in sheet-metal troughs with water outlets at their lowest points (see figure 40). Rainwater therefore drains down between the slabs, through the gravel beds and out via the base outlets.

Assessment
The Farnsworth House expresses to near perfection Mies van der Rohe's belief in an architecture of austere beauty, free of historical allusion or rhetoric, relying on clean forms and noble materials to epitomize an impersonal 'will of the age' that stands aloof from such ephemeralities as fashion or the personal likes and dislikes of individual clients.[74] In its very perfection, by these exalted criteria, lie the building's great strengths but also its weaknesses.

The first strength is its success as a *place*, where the house goes far towards realizing that vision of the dwelling as a spiritual space expressed three decades earlier by Ebeling,[75] and again in 1951 (the very year of its completion) in a noteworthy essay by the German philosopher Heidegger.[76]

The manner in which man, architecture and nature have been brought together on this riverside meadow creates a magical sense of being within nature, not separated from it as in traditional buildings. From their glass-enclosed belvedere residents may tranquilly observe the surrounding meadow and trees change character as one season gives way to the next, the woodland colours heightened by the white framing, and the hourly fluctuations of light subtly reflecting off the white ceiling.

As Peter Carter (who has stayed in the Farnsworth House in all seasons) has observed:

'In summer the great room floats above a green meadow, its visual boundaries extending to the leafy screen of deciduous trees encircling the house, and the high sun bouncing off the travertine surface of the covered terrace to wash the ceiling with a glowing luminosity. On sunny days the white steel profiles receive bright articulation and precise modelling from the sun's rays; on dull days the diffuse light will still pick out the profiles of these architectural elements even when viewed from far away in the meadow. Summer is also the season of truly operatic storms: when witnessed from the glass-walled interior high winds, torrential rain and chunky hail, accompanied by deafening thunder and spectacularly dramatic lightning, leave an indelible impression of nature's more aggressive aspect.

'In autumn the green turns to a golden glow, to be followed by the enchantment of winter when the prairy becomes white-blanketed for weeks on end, the snow lit by a low sun and the bare trees affording long views across the frozen Fox river. By day the slanting sunlight is reflected from the snowy surface on to and into the house, projecting images of nature on to the folds of the curtains and creating a softly luminous interior ambience; by night the glittering snow reflects bright moonlight into the house, mysteriously diminishing the boundary between

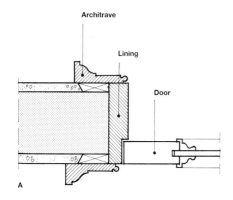

A

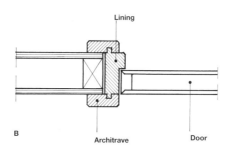

B

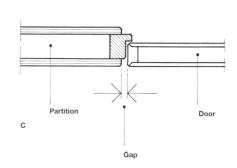

C

42b

42 Doors showing **A** traditional detailing, **B** 1920s Miesian detailing and **C** 1950s Miesian detailing

43 At night the transparent pavilion becomes like a glowing lantern

the man-made interior and the natural world outside.

'As winter passes the landscape becomes alive with the fresh colours and fragrances of spring foliage, the latter slowly closing in once again to define the secluded domain of the home meadow.'

The diurnal cycle is as delightful. Of the sleeping area to the east, a guest who stayed the night wrote that 'the sensation is indescribable – the act of waking and coming to consciousness as the light dawns and gradually grows. It illuminates the grass and trees and the river beyond; it takes over your whole vision. You are in nature and not in it, engulfed by it but separate from it. It is altogether unforgettable.'[77] Another frequent visitor adds: 'The sunrise, of course, is ravishing. But the night as well, especially during thunderstorms. Snowfalls are magical. And I recall times when the river water rose almost to the level of the floor, but not quite, so that we had to locomote by canoe ... I cannot recall a dull moment here.'[78]

In sum: 'For those who have been fortunate enough to live in it the healing qualities of the Farnsworth House confirm its status as the nonpareil of country retreats.' (Peter Carter)

The second great strength of the Farnsworth House is its perfection as an *artefact*. Steel, glass and travertine have been integrated into a classical composition in which everything looks right, from overall form down to the tiniest detail. The result stands as an object lesson for all designers, and the core of the lesson is that excellence cannot be achieved without an insistence on fine materials, consummate details and unremitting design effort. This is especially true of 'honest' modern design, in which components and joints are nakedly displayed as in a Greek temple. Unlike traditional buildings, whose complex mouldings and overlapping finishes and coverings may conceal a host of imperfections, the clarity of such design allows few hiding places, and it requires a Miesian drive for perfection to achieve the results seen at Plano.[79]

Turning to weaknesses, the case against the Farnsworth House is that it pretends to be what it is not in three respects: as an exemplar of industrial materials and construction methods; as an exemplar of rational problem-solving design; and as a reproducible 'type-form' that might be widely adopted for other dwellings – all of these being self-proclaimed aims of Miesian design.[80]

On the first point, the Farnsworth House uses rolled steel sections and plate glass to present itself as a model of industrial-age construction when in fact it is an expensive artwork fabricated largely by handcraft. A case for the defence was suggested in 1960 by the architect and critic Peter Blake: that in an age of throw-away products and, increasingly, throw-away architecture, Mies was legitimately creating prototypes that the construction industry of the future might strive to emulate; that he saw his role as that of directing the course of industry, not slavishly following it.[81] Forty years on it looks as though Mies may yet be vindicated – industrial technology is producing objects of increasing perfection, and moving away from standardized towards customized production; and twenty-first-century industry could conceivably become capable of delivering buildings of Miesian quality at normal cost.

On the second charge, it is undeniable that the Farnsworth House suffers from serious and elementary design faults. It was perfectly predictable that a badly-ventilated glass box, without sun-shading except for some nearby trees, would become oven-like in the hot Illinois summers, and that single-thickness glass in steel frames, devoid of precautionary measures such as convection heaters to sweep the glass with a warm air current, would stream with condensation in an Illinois winter. Mies's disregard of such elementary truths illustrates his greatest weakness as an architect – namely, an obsession with perfect form so single-minded that awkward problems were loftily disregarded.[82]

That brings us to the third of the points raised above – whether the Farnsworth House might serve as a reproducible 'type-form'. It seems clear that Mies intended the concept of the Farnsworth House for wider application. His broadly similar 50 ft by 50 ft (15m × 15m) House project of 1950–1, which he reportedly thought suitable for mass-production for American family housing,[83] was open-plan and glass-walled, and shared with the 55 ft by 29 ft (16.8m × 8.8m) Farnsworth House a lack of privacy, lack of storage space, and very little adaptability apart from the occupants' freedom to move the furniture. For normal living these are crippling defects.

Though Mies insisted to the end of his days that open interiors were practical and preferable to conventional rooms,[84] this cannot possibly be true for dwellings unless they are large enough to ensure privacy by distance – which means very large indeed: it is significant that the over 80 ft × 50 ft (24m × 15m)

43

44

open-plan living room of the successful Tugendhat House is three-and-a-half times the size of an entire floor of the Riehl House or Perls House. As to storage space, it is difficult to imagine a family inhabiting the 50 ft by 50 ft house – or even the 60 ft × 60 ft (18m × 18m) version – when the bachelor aesthete Philip Johnson's 56 ft by 32 ft (17m × 9.8m) single-space 1949 Glass House at New Canaan depended on the existence of several nearby buildings to which possessions, guests and other intrusions of everyday life could be conveniently banished. In this connection Peter Blake writes that the traditional Japanese open plan that so inspired Frank Lloyd Wright and other twentieth-century architects depended absolutely, even in that age of sparse possessions, on servants and subservient wives constantly spiriting away the clutter of everyday living into special areas outside the open plan.[85]

Clearly the Farnsworth House fails as a normal dwelling, and as a prototype for normal dwellings. But turning to happier things, it undeniably provides a supreme model for a belvedere, a garden pavilion or even a holiday dwelling, provided the client truly understands what he or she is getting, as the unfortunate Dr Farnsworth probably did not. One of the contractors on her house, Karl Freund, later told the writer David Spaeth, 'she didn't understand the house. Mies should have made it clearer to her what she was getting.'[86] Buildings very obviously inspired by the Farnsworth House include the 1970 Tallon House in Dublin, Ireland by Ronnie Tallon; the 1992 Villa Maesen at Zedelgem, Belgium by Stéphane Beel; and the 1998 Skywood House in Middlesex, England by Graham Phillips.[87]

In sum: the crystalline masterpiece on the riverside at Plano is a rare building for a rare client, to be emulated selectively and with very great care.

Postscript

In 1971 Dr Edith Farnsworth vacated the famous pavilion that had become so deeply intertwined with her life and would always bear her name. Her original devotion to the house had evaporated in the quarrel with Mies: she never furnished it properly and angrily discouraged visits. She had nevertheless continued to own and use it until finally demoralized by a new misfortune.

In the 1960s the Board of Supervisors of Kendall County decided to widen and re-align the road and bridge along the western boundary of the site. These works required the purchase of a 60m (200 ft) wide strip of Dr Farnsworth's land, a proposal she vigorously contested. There followed a painful battle with the County authority, culminating in a court hearing after which the ground was compulsorily purchased. In 1967 the authorities built a new road that was twice the width of the old, raised on an embankment, 45m (150 ft) closer to the house and clearly visible therefrom. The traffic was now faster and noisier than before, and audible from the house.

The once quiet and secluded retreat was no longer quite so magical, and in 1968 Dr Farnsworth advertised it for sale. Thus, with tragic symmetry, her twenty-year occupation of a house she had commissioned with love and enthusiasm ended as it had begun – with a traumatic court hearing ending in defeat.[88]

The offer to sell came to the notice of Mr Peter (now Lord) Palumbo, a London property developer and lover of modern architecture with a particular respect for the works of Mies van der Rohe. Knowing of Dr Farnsworth's severe reputation he risked entering the grounds to look at the house, and decided at once that he must buy. Taking his life in his hands, as he put it, he knocked on the door. 'I essentially bought the house that afternoon', he later recalled, 'but she was a difficult, ferocious woman and we didn't really complete the deal until 1972.'

Lord Palumbo's original dream that Mies van der Rohe might be commissioned to restore to perfection his own twenty-year-old building was cruelly thwarted when the latter died in 1969. The commission was therefore given in 1972 to Dirk Lohan, Mies's grandson and a partner in Conterato, Fugikawa and Lohan, the successor-office to Mies's atelier.[89]

The principal works required were the following.[90]

With respect to structure, the flat roof (an inherently trouble-

44 Kitchen detail

45 The bathroom in the core area of the house. Here the primavera-faced plywood panels have been painted white with waterproof paint

prone form of construction in cold climates[91]) had deteriorated quite badly: condensation had caused staining, bubbling and cracking of the plastered underside, and the paint finish on the latter had begun to peel away. To improve its performance a vapour barrier was installed above the plaster, additional insulation laid above the pre-cast concrete planks, and a new waterproof membrane laid on the upper surface. On the underside the damaged plaster and paint were replaced.

The mosquito screens were removed from the terrace, the white finish to all steelwork was stripped back to the primer coat and repainted, and all the glass panels were replaced.

With respect to services, all the existing installations received a major overhaul. The original space-heating principles (floor-embedded coils for main heating, augmented by fan-induced hot air for quick warming-up) were left unchanged, but the oil-fired heating system, which was dirty and cumbersome, was converted to electricity. All the wiring in the house was replaced. The 'almost nothing' hearth with its propensity for spreading ash was given a travertine platform. Air-conditioning (a rare luxury when the Farnsworth House was designed in the 1940s) was newly installed, and the plant concealed above the service core.

And finally the interior, which Dr Farnsworth had filled with a miscellany of inappropriate articles (see for instance the photo on p.21 of Schulze, *The Farnsworth House*), was at last furnished as first intended. Her roller blinds were replaced with off-white curtains as envisaged by Mies, and the prosaic furniture replaced by a few classic pieces placed almost as sparingly and precisely as exhibits in an art gallery. The black glass table with chrome legs seen near the entrance in some published photographs is a rare survivor of the Barcelona Pavilion.

Turning from the building to its setting, Lord Palumbo immediately removed the crazy-paving pathway to the front steps and put in hand a gradual improvement programme for the entire site, which had been neglected for twenty years.

During her ownership Dr Farnsworth had bought an additional 55 acres of land to the east of the original seven-acre site, creating the potential for a relocated and more discreet car access route. Now Lord Palumbo commissioned the American garden designer Lanning Roper, a devotee of informal English garden design, to replan the landscape substantially.

In its original state the house looked out east, north and west on terrain with grassland, natural shrub and a scattering of trees. At first Lord Palumbo tried to enhance the sense of unspoilt nature by allowing the grass surrounding the Farnsworth House to grow tall, in effect creating a meadow. But the long grass proved difficult to cut and became a fertile breeding-ground for mosquitoes. The grass is now regularly mown, with the cutters set at their highest level.

Lanning Roper planted trees to the east and west, leaving the space directly behind and north of the house as a tract of lawn that slopes lazily upward toward River Road. 'This open space he filled with daffodils, literally tens of thousands of them, which blossom progressively in the spring, leaving the ground decorated with patches of yellow and white. The moment of bloom is brief but compelling, and the landscape hardly less compelling later, when the flowers give way to a meadow wholly of summery green.'[92]

The new stands of trees to the north, east and west now provide an enclosure for the house and the scenic backdrop that is seen through the transparent walls.

Roper also replanned the access route, moving the access gate nearly 200m (650 ft) to the east of the original, out of sight of the house, and laying a gravel drive that sweeps gently round from the north to terminate in a new parking area 45m (150 ft) from the south-eastern corner of the house. When visitors arrive at this riverside parking space they leave their cars, cross a modest timber bridge that arches over a small stream, and make their way to towards the house through a landscape dotted with trees. There is no pathway across the meadow, so that the house is gradually revealed through the foliage.

The new approach, which involves walking the full length of the house before turning at right angles towards the flight of access steps, has therefore become more dramatic than the simple 'house in a meadow' arrangement created by Mies.[93]

The above improvements deserve high praise, but many visitors have felt that the road realignments by Kendall County, the designation of the opposite river bank as a public park, and the creation of relatively lawn-like grass in place of the original untended meadow, have combined to transform an isolated retreat into what is essentially a suburban house – a depressing fate shared by several other icons of twentieth-century architecture including

45

1 River Road
2 Plano Milbrook Road (1951)
3 Fox River Drive (today)
4 Trees
5 Garage built by Dr Farnsworth
6 Original site boundary
7 New parking area added by Lord Palumbo
8 Fox River

Approximate heights above river level:

Farnsworth House floor 15 ft (4.6m)
Contour A (high water mark for a few days every year) 14ft (4.3m)
Contour B (high water mark when the ice breaks up) 16ft (4.9m)
Contour C (high water mark during the 1996 flood) 20ft (6.0m)

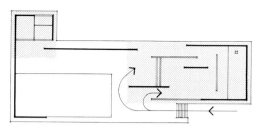

47

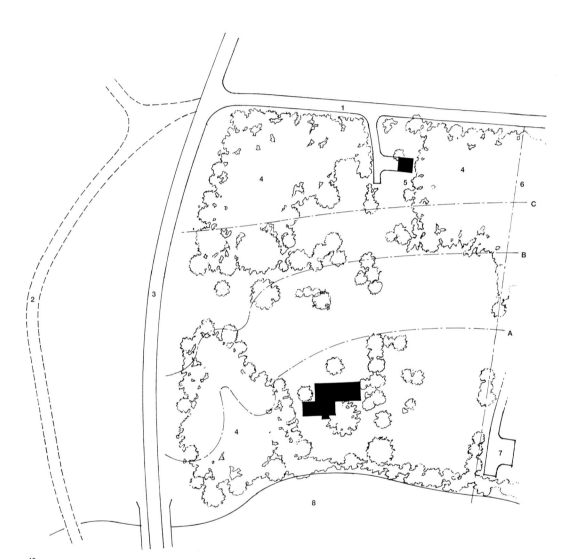

46

Le Corbusier's Villa Savoye and Frank Lloyd Wright's Taliesin West.

A worse development has been a steep rise in the flood-levels of the Fox River. Mies van der Rohe's enquiries in 1946 established a maximum water level over the past century of about 0.9m (3 ft) above ground-level, and he considered it safe to locate the floor 1.6m (5 ft 3 in) above the plain. But, partly as a result of the outward expansion and paving-over of Chicago's environs, the volume of water run-off increased and flood levels began to rise dramatically in the 1950s.

In 1954, three years after Dr Farnsworth moved in, the spring flood rose 1.2m (4 ft) above the pavilion floor. Carpets and furniture were ravaged but the water-marked wooden core unit was fortunately reparable.

In 1996 came a truly gigantic downpour, with 0.45m (18 in) of rain falling in 24 hours, most of it in eight hours. The resulting floodwaters broke two of the glass walls, rose 1.5m (5 ft) above the pavilion floor, swept away artefacts, and ruined not only carpets and furniture but also the wood-veneer finish to the core. An unpleasant layer of mud and silt covered the travertine floor and the damage came to over $500,000.

As Lord Palumbo has put it, the house had to be 'taken apart and put together again', and Dirk Lohan, now of the architectural firm Lohan Associates, was commissioned to carry out the necessary restoration.[94] The timber core unit was so badly damaged that it had to be discarded and built anew. As the once-plentiful primavera was now almost

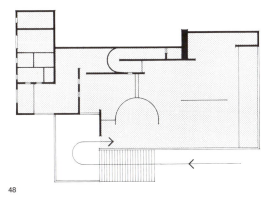

48

46	The Farnsworth site as in 2002
47	Approach route to the Barcelona Pavilion – see n.93
48	Approach route to the Tugendhat House
49	The Farnsworth House semi-submerged during the exceptional 1996 flood; and
50	poised a foot or so above water during one of the more normal floods

extinct Dirk Lohan had to search for months to find wood of the original colour. The new plywood panels were attached to their frames by clips rather than screws so that the panels could be quickly dismantled and stored on top of the core unit in case of flood.

In February 1997, even before the above restoration had started, there was yet another flood, rising to only 0.30 m (1 ft) above floor level but confirming that the Farnsworth House must henceforth survive in conditions very different from those for which it had been designed. There has been talk of installing jacks beneath the footings, able to lift the entire structure in case of flood, but this phenomenally expensive solution remains conjectural. Since buying the house Lord Palumbo has spent roughly $1 million on repairs and improvements, mostly in restoration work after the floods of 1996 and 1997, and one can understand a pause for deliberation. These days the water regularly rises two or three steps above the lower terrace, and occasionally a foot or so above internal floor level, bringing in a layer of silt but not (so far) causing ruin.

Despite the double irony that a dwelling designed as a private retreat is now open to the public, and that its survival is being threatened by the element it was specifically designed to surmount, this chronicle can nevertheless end on an uplifting note. Mies van der Rohe's glass pavilion, having survived fifty troubled years, has become one of the most revered buildings of the twentieth century, constantly visited by admirers from all over the world.

49

50

Photographs

Previous page Approaching the Farnsworth House. The vertical stacking of free-floating horizontal planes first seen in Mies's unbuilt Glass Skyscraper and Concrete Office projects of 1922 and 1923 is here realized, though at a much smaller scale. The idea has since become deeply embedded in modern design

This page The open terrace at the western end of the house

Opposite The dining area, looking west towards the terrace

Two eastward views from the living zone, past the kitchen to the sleeping area at the far end

The sleeping area at the eastern end, where the sleeper awakes to the glory of the rising sun. As in the rest of the house, privacy can be obtained by drawing off-white curtains across the glass walls. The hopper windows below right are the only opening lights in the entire building

Left An eastward view along the living zone towards the sleeping area at the far end. On the left is the somewhat ineffective fireplace
Below A closer view of the Mies-designed chair and table seen in the middle distance at left

The south-eastern corner of the house and two close-up views, showing how white-painted steel, glass and travertine have been immaculately conjoined. Note the complete absence of visible bolts or welds: components appear to be held together by a kind of magnetism

The Farnsworth House snowbound in the severe Illinois winter (far left), in autumn and (below) in summer. It is a curious feature of this building that photographs almost invariably diminish its true scale. The top of the porch floor, below, is approximately at the eye-level of an average-height person standing beside it

Location map
scale 1:1250

Drawings

Floor plan
scale 1:200

1 terrace
2 porch
3 kitchen
4 shower room
5 bathroom
6 boiler room
7 fireplace

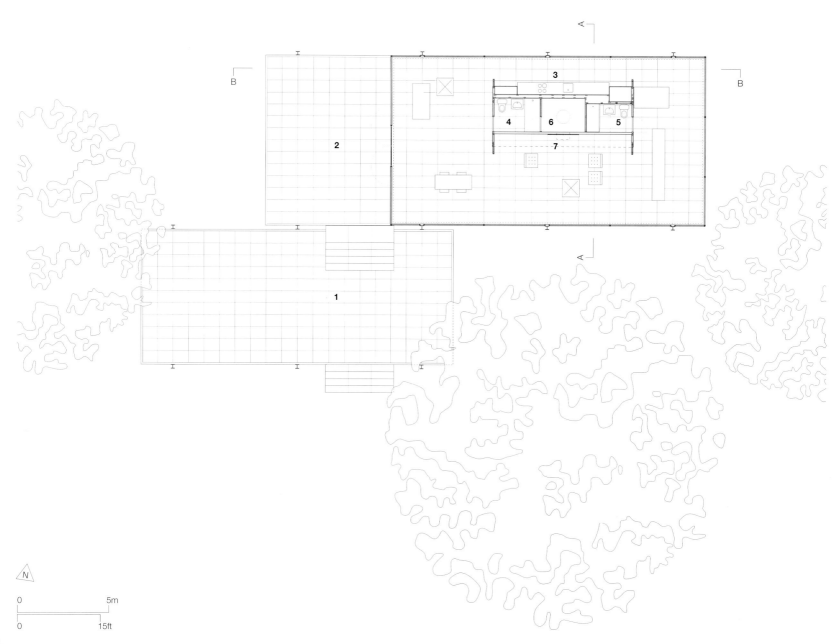

Section and elevation
scale 1:100

1 terrace
2 bathroom
3 kitchen

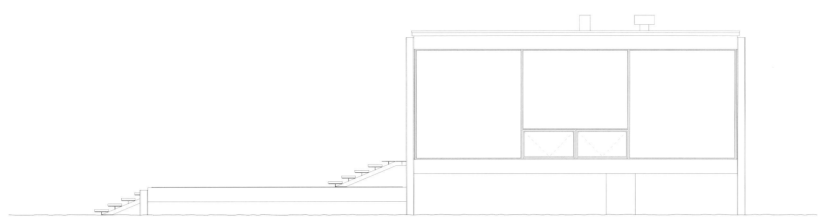

East elevation

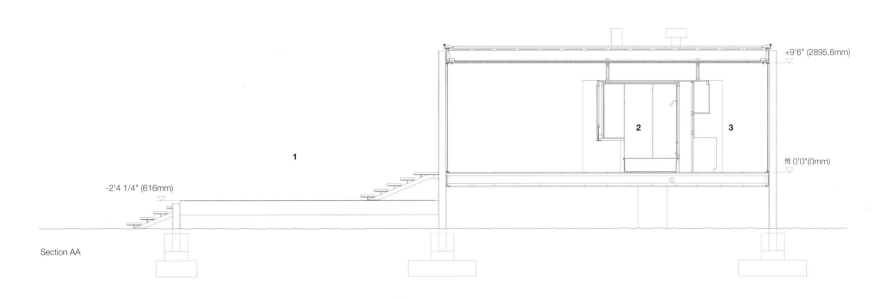

Section AA

Section and elevations
scale 1:100

1 terrace
2 porch
3 kitchen

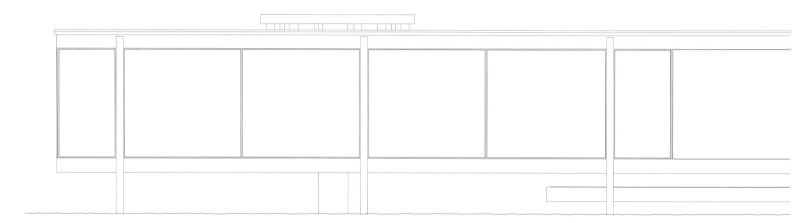

North elevation

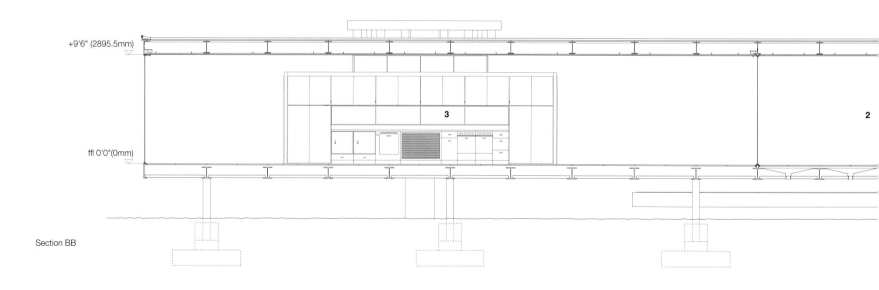

Section BB

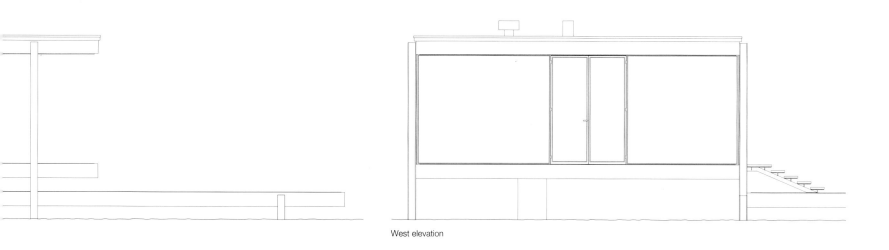
West elevation

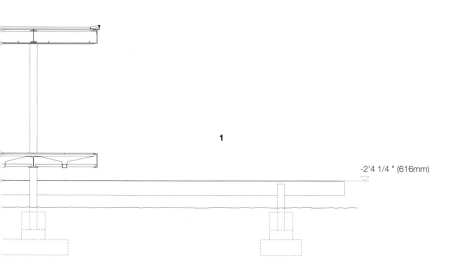
-2'4 1/4 " (616mm)

Core plan
scale 1:50

1 shower room
2 travertine shower floor
3 boiler room
4 utility stack
5 chimney flue
6 extract fan
7 bathroom
8 kitchen
9 plywood lining
10 drain

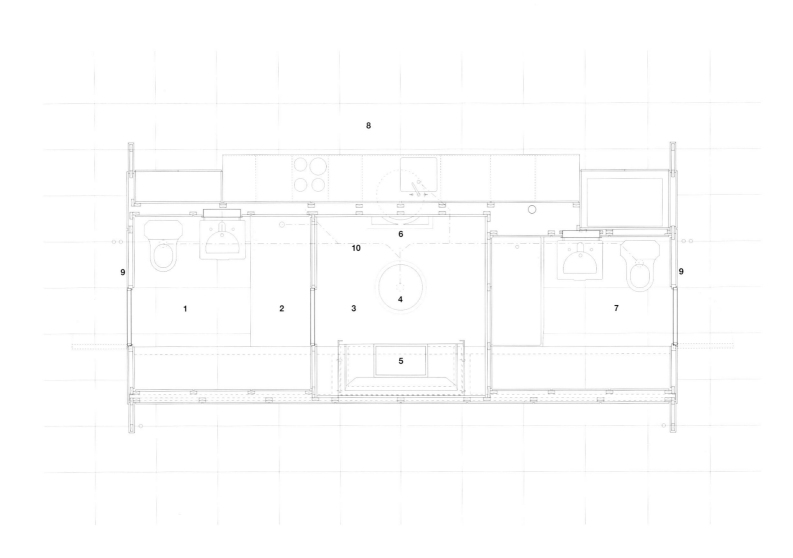

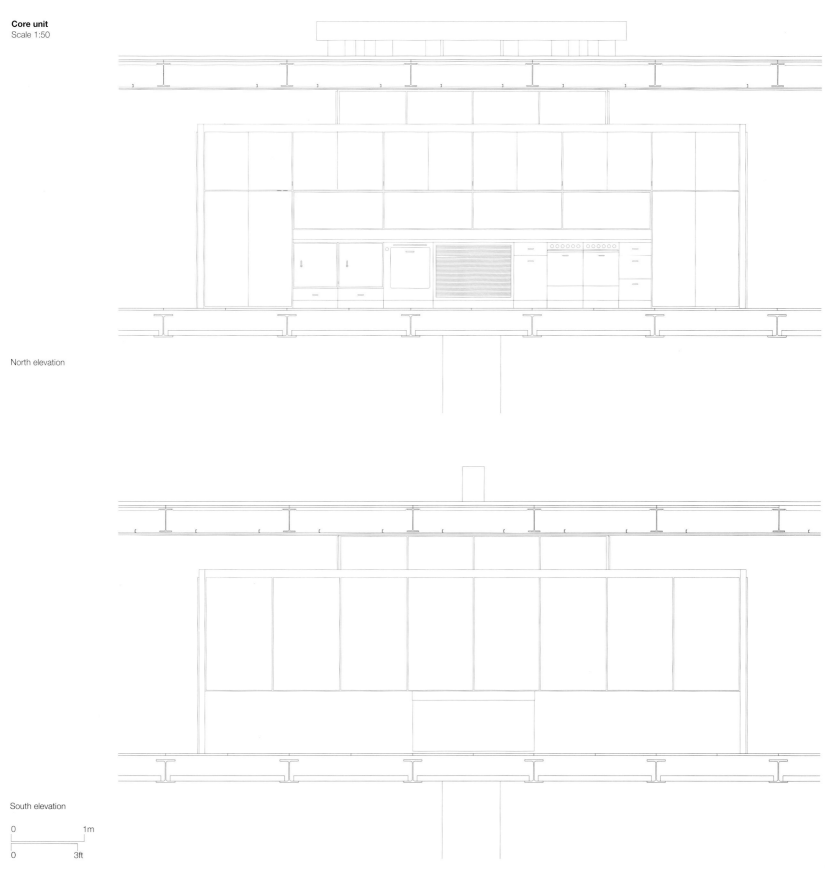

Core unit
Scale 1:50

North elevation

South elevation

0 — 1m
0 — 3ft

Key to details
scale 1:200

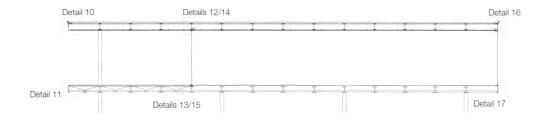

Section XX

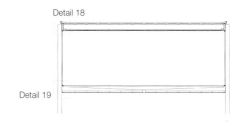

Section YY

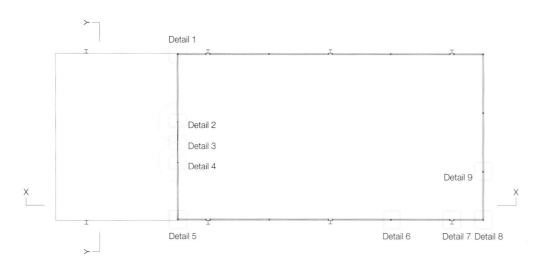

Plan

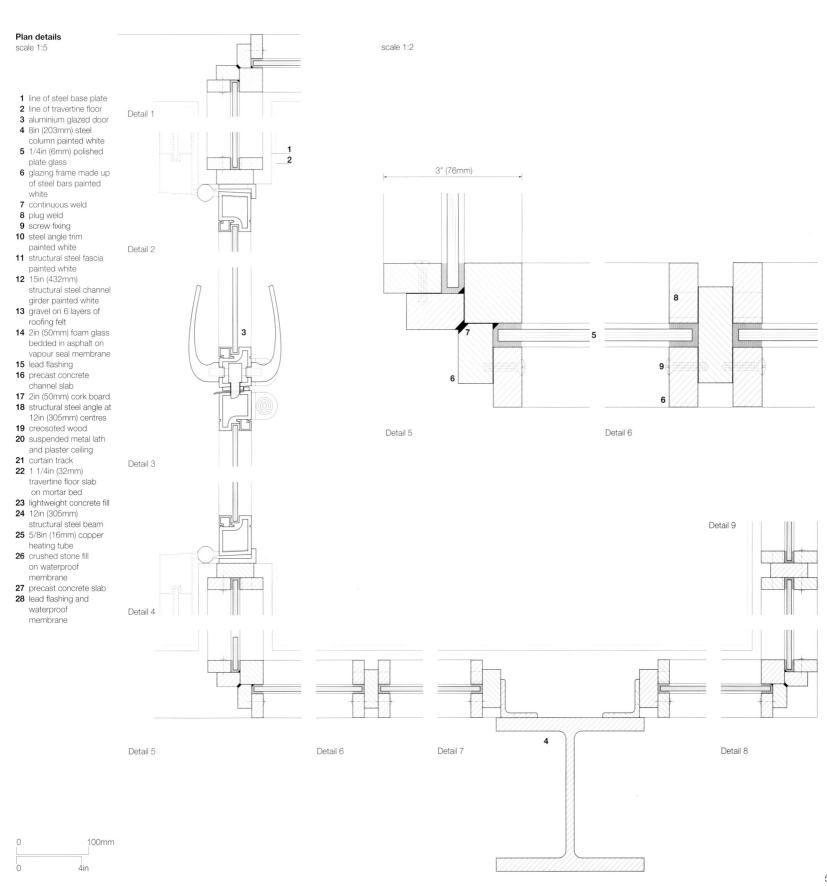

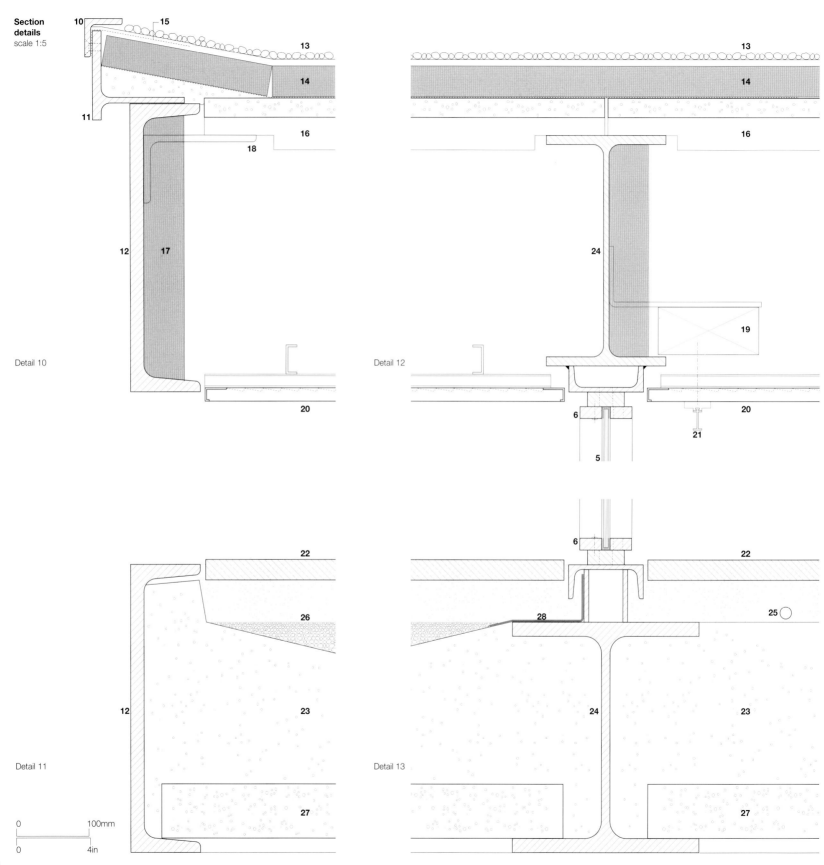

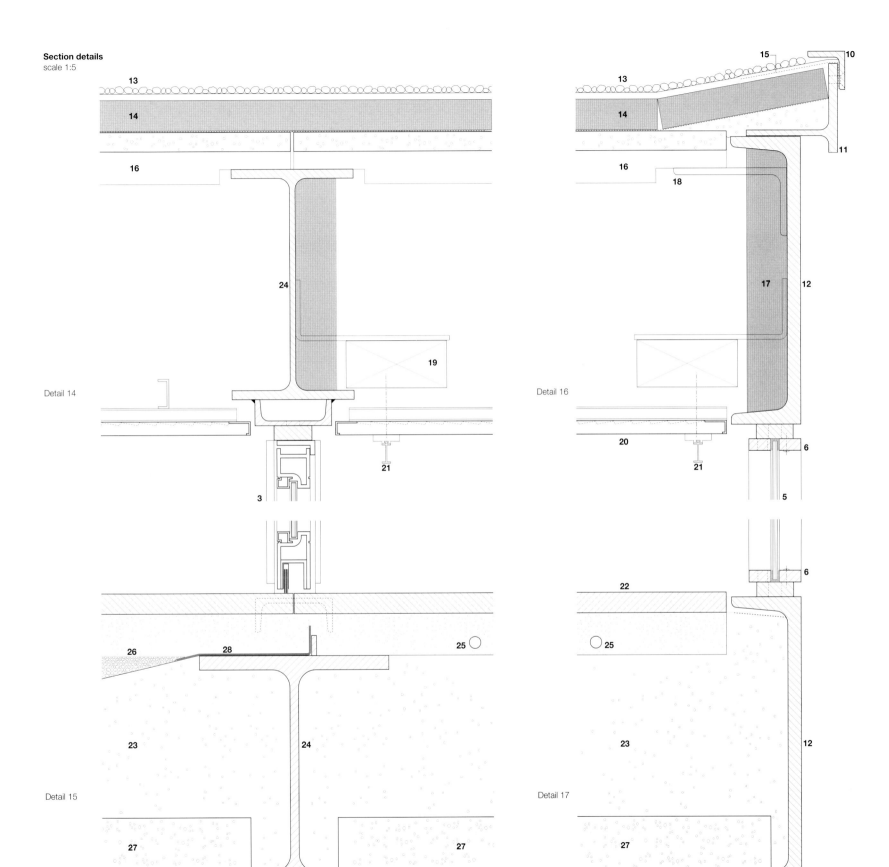

Section details
scale 1:5

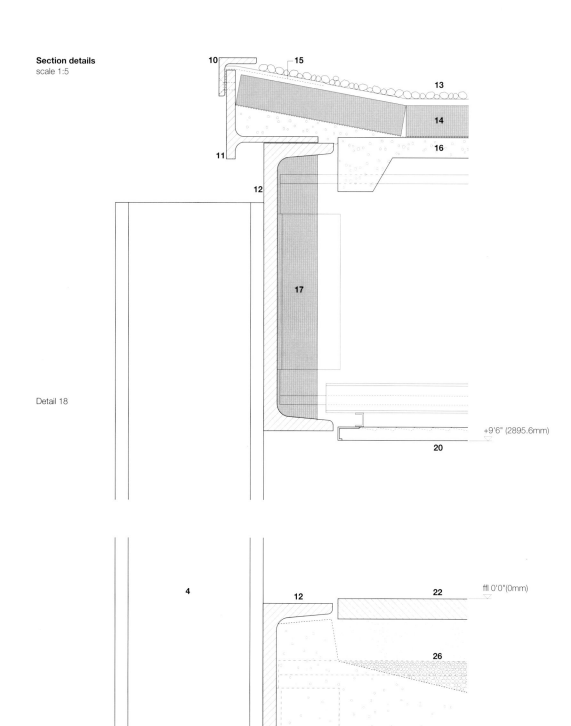

Detail 18

Detail 19

1 line of steel base plate
2 line of travertine floor
3 aluminium glazed door
4 8in (203mm) steel column painted white
5 1/4in (6mm) polished plate glass
6 glazing frame made up of steel bars painted white
7 continuous weld
8 plug weld
9 screw fixing
10 steel angle trim painted white
11 structural steel fascia painted white
12 15in (432mm) structural steel channel girder painted white
13 gravel on 6 layers of roofing felt
14 2in (50mm) foam glass bedded in asphalt on vapour seal membrane
15 lead flashing
16 precast concrete channel slab
17 2in (50mm) cork board
18 structural steel angle at 12in (305mm) centres
19 creosoted wood
20 suspended metal lath and plaster ceiling
21 curtain track
22 1 1/4in (32mm) travertine floor slab on mortar bed
23 lightweight concrete fill
24 12in (305mm) structural steel beam
25 5/8in (16mm) copper heating tube
26 crushed stone fill on waterproof membrane
27 precast concrete slab
28 lead flashing and waterproof membrane

NOTES

Mies van der Rohe is quoted in many books, especially those by Philip Johnson and Peter Carter (see Select Bibliography). But in the interests of consistency I have, wherever possible, sourced such quotations to *The Artless Word* by Fritz Neumeyer, which reproduces and dates Mies's key texts and lectures with particular clarity.

1. From Henry-Russell Hitchcock and Arthur Drexler, *Built in USA: Post-war Architecture*. New York: Simon and Schuster, 1952; pp.20–1
2. The country villa originates in Roman times, but our knowledge of these is imperfect. Better known are Palladio's sixteenth-century dwellings in and around the Veneto, and eighteenth-century derivatives by architects such as Colen Campbell and Lord Burlington. For a history from antiquity to Le Corbusier's Villa Savoye see James S Ackerman's *The Villa*, London: Thames and Hudson, 1990. The villa is a peculiarly important building type because idealized house designs, both built and unbuilt, have long been used to express new architectural paradigms – see Peter Collins in *Changing Ideals in Modern Architecture*, London: Faber, 1965, pp.42–58
3. Unlike the villa (from Latin 'rural house'), the modest countryside cabin is not a formal architectural type. But there are notable architect-designed examples, two of which (figs. 2 and 3) confirm that the framed cabin, raised on stilts above a watery site, was a known model that was classicized and refined rather than invented by Mies van der Rohe in 1946–51. The first, Walter Gropius and Marcel Breuer's H G Chamberlain House in Wayland, MA, was built in 1940 and was probably known to Mies. The second, Paul Rudolph and Ralph Twitchell's Healy Guest House in Florida, was almost contemporary with the Farnsworth House, being designed and built in 1948–50. A more general influence might have been Le Corbusier's many stilted 'boxes up in the air', whose underlying motive is interestingly discussed in Adolf Max Vogt's *Le Corbusier: the Noble Savage*. Cambridge, MA/London: MIT Press, 1998
4. All his working life Mies 'read widely and pondered the basic questions of human existence and their implications for architecture'. In 1961 he was still insisting that 'only questions into the essence of things are meaningful …' (Neumeyer p.30)
5. Carter p.174
6. Ibid. p.174
7. Ford p.263
8. Carter p.10
9. From 'Mies in Berlin', an interview recorded on a gramophone disc in 1966 and issued by Bauwelt Archiv, Berlin. A translated extract was published under the title 'Mies Speaks' in the *Architectural Review*, London, Dec 1968, pp.451–2
10. When in 1908 Mies joined the studio of Peter Behrens (1868–1940) it was one of the most exciting practices in Germany, attracting such future stars as the young Gropius (in 1907–10) and Le Corbusier (in 1910–11). Having been a leading exponent of Art Nouveau, Behrens began in 1903 to search for a design approach less superficial and subjective, and arguably more suited to the needs of an industrial society. This led him to the works of Schinkel (1781–1841) whose noble boulevards, squares and buildings were prominent features of early twentieth-century Berlin. Behrens' work from about 1905 onwards became sober, massive and powerful, and he had a seminal role in developing the new forms of modern architecture. A prime example is the proto-modern AEG Turbine Factory (1909) with its innovative and powerfully expressive shape, and its glassy side walls and clearly-exhibited steel frames.
11. 'In the Altes Museum [Schinkel] has separated the windows very clearly, he separated the elements, the columns and the walls and the ceiling, and I think that is still visible in my later buildings' – Mies talking to Graeme Shankland on the BBC Third Programme, 1959 (Carter p.182). In fact this kind of clarity was already visible in Mies's Riehl House (see Schulze, *Mies van der Rohe*, p.28) and Schinkel's role may have been to confirm and enhance a sensibility that was already present in the young Mies.
12. Mies's view was that architectural form should result from the nature of the problem to be solved, and not from preconceived style. He expressed this often, from the 1920s – 'Form is not the goal but the result of our work' (Neumeyer pp.242, 243, 247, 257) – until the 1950s when he still insisted that 'architecture has nothing to do with the invention of forms' and that 'the invention of forms is obviously not the task of the building art' (Neumeyer pp.324–5). But he was one of the great form-givers of the age, imposing upon project after project his own twentieth-century distillations of the forms of classical architecture, often in defiance of structural logic.
13. See n.9
14. For early examples of Mies allowing appearance to determine structure, rather than vice versa, see the Esters and Lange houses (1927–30): their very long window lintels, invisibly supported by hidden steel beams, are exceptionally neat but contradict the nature of load-bearing brickwork. Mies's pavilions in the Bacardi Office Building project (1957) and New National Gallery (1962–7) are late examples: as Peter Blundell Jones has pointed out their forms are virtually identical despite the fact that the first was meant to be made of concrete and the second of welded steel. For examples of buildings in which structure truly does determine form one must go to the very un-Miesian Antoni Gaudi, whose organic-looking Colonia Guell Chapel (1898–1914) has inward-leaning columns which follow experimentally-derived stress lines instead of western classical verticality.
15. In 1952 Mies told students that it was thanks to Peter Behrens that he had developed a feeling for 'grand form' and a 'sense of the monumental' (Tegethoff p.26). In 1961 he told Peter Carter that 'Peter Behrens had a marvellous feeling for form … and it is this feeling for form that I learned from him …' (Neumeyer p.352). In 1966 he said in a recorded interview (n.9) that 'under Behrens I learned the grand form.'
16. Mies was self-confessedly influenced by Frank Lloyd Wright. He later wrote: 'Toward the beginning of the twentieth century the great revival of architecture in Europe, instigated by William Morris, began to … lose force. Distinct signs of exhaustion became manifest.' By 1910, he went on, 'we younger architects found ourselves in painful inner conflict'. Then there came to Berlin an exhibition of the work of Frank Lloyd Wright. 'The work of this great master revealed an architectural world of unexpected force and clarity of language … The more deeply we studied Wright's creations, the greater became our admiration for his incomparable talent … The dynamic impulse emanating from his work invigorated a whole generation.' (Neumeyer p.321)
17. Avant-garde architectural and artistic movements in Berlin during the time Mies worked there included Expressionism from Germany, De Stijl from the Netherlands and Constructivism and Suprematism from Russia. There were also vigorously propagandist organizations such

as the leftist Novembergruppe (November Group) of which Mies was a member; Die Gläserne Kette (Glass Chain) of which he was not; and publications such as *Gestaltung* ('Form-giving') which he helped to found and to which he contributed. For a summary of these influences see Neumeyer pp.15–27; and for brief descriptions of the movements see *The Thames and Hudson Encyclopaedia of 20th Century Architecture*, London: Thames and Hudson, 1983

18 It is difficult today to imagine how wholly unprecedented and revelatory this project was. The massiveness of traditional building had suddenly been replaced by an alternative whose sheer glass facades gave full expression to Bruno Taut's exultant cry in the first issue of the Expressionist journal *Frühlicht* in 1920: 'High the transparent, the clear! High purity! High the crystal! ...' (Neumeyer p.3). Alas, in addition to a crystalline glassiness and structural clarity this design also introduced the banal flat top that would come to have such a catastrophic effect on urban skylines the world over – see for comparison the Chicago Tribune Tower design by Raymond Hood and John Mead Howells (1924).

19 The traditional Japanese interior influenced Western design at the turn of the century, partly as a result of the 1893 World's Columbian Exposition in Chicago. The Exposition exhibited a Japanese pavilion whose relatively open interior, divided by light screens rather than walls, came as a revelation to many architects – including 25-year-old Frank Lloyd Wright. This influence is clearly visible in Wright's post-1893 house plans (see Kevin Nute, *Frank Lloyd Wright and Japan*, London: Chapman and Hall, 1993, pp.48–72). His designs were published in 1910–11 by the German publisher Wasmuth as a portfolio titled *Ausgeführte Bauten und Entwürfe*. They had an immense impact on many European architects, including Mies (see n.16). The original portfolio has recently been republished in reduced facsimile as *Studies and Executed Buildings by Frank Lloyd Wright*, London: Architectural Press, 1986.

20 In De Stijl design there were 'no more closed volumes ... There are six planes: the ceiling, four walls, and the floor. Separate the joinings, keeping the planes free; then light will penetrate even the darkest corners of the room, and its space will take on a new life ... Once the planes are separate and independent they can be separated beyond the perimeter of the old box and spread out, go up or down, and reach out beyond the limits that used to cut off the interior from the exterior ... Once the box has been dismembered, the planes no longer form closed volumes ... Instead the rooms become fluid, and join up, and flow ...' (Bruno Zevi in *The Modern Language of Architecture*, Seattle: University of Washington Press, 1978, p.31).

21 The complete absence of doors in the Brick Country House project was a literal intention, and not just a simplification of draughtsmanship, as Mies confirmed: 'I have abandoned the usual concept of closed rooms and striven for a series of spatial effects rather than a row of individual rooms.' (Neumeyer p.250)

22 The open-plan, glass-walled house emerges in Mies's House for a Childless Couple at the 1931 Berlin Building Exposition, the Gericke House project of 1932 and the sequence of Court House projects from 1931–8. These projects are briefly described in Schulze, *Mies van der Rohe* and more extensively in Tegethoff.

23 See n.19

24 The pavilion functioned only to symbolize the openness and freedom of the 1919–33 Weimar Republic, and to cast a spell of tranquillity upon its visitors. It was formally used only once, for an opening ceremony when the Commissioner General of the Republic, Georg von Schnitzler, is reported to have said: 'Here you see the spirit of the new Germany: simplicity and clarity of means and intentions all open to the wind as well as to freedom ... A work made of honesty, without pride. Here is the peaceful house of an appeased Germany.' (A contemporary paraphrase of the speech, by Rubio Tuduri, quoted by Robin Evans, *Translations from Drawing to Building and other Essays*, London: Architectural Association, 1997, p.236). The pavilion's lack of specific function is confirmed in 'Mies Speaks' (n.9).

25 Mies's admiration of the steel skeleton goes back at least as far as 1922, when he wrote of unclad skyscraper structures that 'the impression of the high-reaching steel skeletons is overpowering'. But, he continued, once the claddings were added 'this impression is completely destroyed; the constructive thought ... is annihilated and frequently smothered ...' (Neumeyer p.240)

26 Mies used the phrase 'skin and bone construction' to describe the clear separation between the load-bearing skeleton (bone) and non-load-bearing claddings (skin) so evident in his post-1921 designs. For his first use of the phrase, in 1923, see Neumeyer p.241.

27 See n.4

28 In his early writings, c.1923, Mies appeared to see the core problem of twentieth-century architecture in terms of technology – new materials, new production methods and increased efficiency. By 1927 his language had changed and he was giving primacy to spiritual values. Thus in 1927 he viewed the housing problem as 'a spiritual problem' (Neumeyer p.258); a year later he wrote that 'building art is always the spatial expression of spiritual decisions' (ibid. p.304); and two years later he expressed a similar sentiment (ibid. p.309).

29 Siegfried Ebeling, a Bauhaus member, published in 1926 a highly mystical (and somewhat mystifying) tract entitled *Der Raum als Membran* or 'Space as Membrane'. Ebeling saw buildings, and the house in particular, as forming a membrane between man and exterior space, creating an interior that 'could do justice to one's relationship with one's body, one's being, and the eternity of the cosmos'. Many might find these notions (which Ebeling propounds at length and in opaque language) overstated, but Mies was in search of transcendental meanings and the underlinings in his copy of *Der Raum* suggest that he took these ideas seriously. Ebeling's ideas are discussed, and their possible influence on Mies's work traced, in Neumeyer pp.171–9. See also n.76 below on Martin Heidegger.

30 All the underlying ideas realized in the Farnsworth House are present in a few sentences written by Mies in 1933. In praise of the possibilities of steel and glass construction he says: 'Only now can we articulate space, open it up and connect it to the landscape, thereby satisfying the spatial needs of modern man. Simplicity of construction, clarity of tectonic means, and purity of material shall be the bearers of a new beauty.' (Neumeyer p.314) For his 1958 declaration to Norberg-Schulz on the restrained use of colour in building interiors see Neumeyer pp.338–9.

31 *Architectural Forum*, October 1951, pp.156–62. The review is highly favourable but balanced: while praising the Farnsworth House's fine qualities, and suggesting that it might be 'the most important house completed in the US since Frank Lloyd Wright completed his desert home in Arizona a dozen years ago', the *Forum* also noted that the house would have 'little to say to those whose ideal is an informal setting for family living', or to those 'who seek first to express the individual personality of a client'.

32 The term 'International Style' was conferred by the American critics Henry-Russell Hitchcock and Philip Johnson upon a strand of European modernism that had crystallized between 1922 and 1932 in a series of buildings by Le Corbusier, Oud, Gropius, Lurçat, Rietveld and Mies (see Hitchcock and Johnson, *The International Style: Architecture since 1922*, New York: W W Norton & Co, 1932 and 1966). These buildings were typically white, cubically or horizontally-composed, strip-windowed or occasionally glass-walled, devoid of ornament, and formed of smooth, thin-looking flat planes rather than massive walls. Indisputably modern designs of somewhat different character were being produced during those years by architects such as Hugo Häring, but the clinical style publicized in Hitchcock and Johnson's book did seem for a while to be the emerging image of modern architecture.

33 Though never becoming popular in American house design, the International Style did dominate American office building design for four decades, starting with Raymond Hood's McGraw-Hill Building (1929–30); Howe and Lescaze's Philadelphia Saving Fund Society Building (1929–32); Pietro Belluschi's Equitable Life Assurance Building (1944–7); Wallace Harrison's United Nations Secretariat Building (1947–50); and Skidmore Owings and Merrill's Lever House (1951–2). In the USA the International Style also lost its European connotations of social improvement and became simply a clean and modern way of shaping buildings. This suited Mies who, despite protestations such as those quoted in n.28, had always shown more enthusiasm for the pursuit of architectonic form than for the radical transformation of society.

34 The variety, inventiveness and warmth of American houses of the late 1930s to early 1950s is seen in the work of Gregory Ain, Edward Larrabee Barnes, Marcel Breuer, Mario Corbett, Charles Eames, Harwell Hamilton Harris, John Johansen, Richard Neutra, Igor Polevitzky, Schweikher and Elting, Paolo Soleri, Raphael Soriano, Ralph S Twitchell and Lloyd Wright in *Built in USA: Post-war Architecture* (see n.1 above). A good short history appears in Jordy pp.165–219.

35 After virtually disappearing from view during the 1920s, the septuagenarian Frank Lloyd Wright swept back to a dominant position in American architecture with Fallingwater (1935–9) and the Johnson Wax administration building (1936–9).

36 'Looking closely at the early Chicago skyscrapers we readily observe the crudity of most of them. Frames and windows are often ill-proportioned. The masonry and terra-cotta sheathing is often clumsy in both its profile and its surface ornamentation. The juncture of one member or one material with another is often awkward. There are, to be sure, fine buildings among these early Chicago skyscrapers. The majority, however, are boldly, vitally, courageously gawky ...' Jordy pp.225–6

37 Including such manifestations of Western geometric discipline as strict adherence to the Cartesian grid (no hint, yet, of the exploded forms of Frank Gehry etc.), a concern for proportion and regular spacing of vertical elements. These continuities are particularly apparent in the work of Mies.

38 Buildings by Mies included in *The International Style* (n.32) were his Apartment Building at the

Weissenhof Siedlung, Stuttgart (1927); German Pavilion at the Barcelona Exposition (1929); Lange House, Krefeld (1928); Tugendhat House, Brno (1930); and Apartment Study, New York (1930). The Tugendhat House was given especial prominence.

39 Mies's later fame tends to obscure the fact that in 1945 he was almost unknown outside Germany. In Europe he had built (besides exhibitions) only six notable houses, two small apartment blocks and a memorial monument; in America only one building, the IIT Minerals and Metal Research Building (1942–3) with Holabird and Root as co-architects. His international reputation began to take off only in 1947, a decade after his arrival in the USA, with publication of Philip Johnson's monograph *Mies van der Rohe*. Johnson's black-and-white images of Mies's clean planar compositions came to many as a revelation of what a truly modern architecture could look like. Mies by this time was over sixty.

40 See *The Farnsworth House*, 1997, written by Franz Schulze (a respected Miesian authority) and produced by Dirk Lohan, Mies's grandson and associate in practice until Mies's death in 1969. This booklet is more recent than most of the standard references, and where different sources give different accounts of events I have assumed it to be the most reliable.

41 See n.24

42 Schulze, *The Farnsworth House*

43 Extracts from the *House Beautiful* article and subsequent polemic may be found in Schulze, *The Farnsworth House*, p.19 and Schulze, *Mies van der Rohe*, p.259.

44 It is interesting and perhaps significant that Le Corbusier's Villa Savoye, which vies with the Farnsworth House for the title of 'second most famous villa of modern architecture' (Frank Lloyd Wright's Fallingwater being first), also generated serious owner dissatisfaction and threats of litigation over defects.

45 See n.43

46 Wright, who seldom praised the work of his contemporaries (particularly if they were European) admitted that he admired Mies's Barcelona Pavilion and Tugendhat House (Schulze, *Mies van der Rohe*, pp.158 and 210). In 1937 he welcomed Mies to Taliesin East for an afternoon visit that became a four-day stay (ibid. p.210–11). The next year he introduced Mies at a formal dinner with the words: 'I admire him as an architect, respect and love him as a man … you treat him well and love him as I do' (ibid. p.219). In 1944 he began to disagree with Mies, dismissing the latter's design for the IIT Library and Administration building as 'a new classicism' (Spaeth p.132), but he was still writing warm personal letters as late as October 1947. (Schulze, *Mies van der Rohe*, pp.237–8)

47 See n.43

48 Schulze, *The Farnsworth House*

49 After the breakdown in their relations, Edith Farnsworth described Mies as 'simply colder and more cruel than anyone I have ever known' – a description not recognized by those who remember the genial, if somewhat taciturn, Mies; while his own version was that 'the lady expected the architect to go along with the house' – a comment unworthy of this normally gallant man. The truth may be that a somewhat lonely woman was yearning for a friend, while her architect wanted only to build a noble building, and that each preferred not to recognize the true motives of the other (see Schulze, *Mies van der Rohe*, p.253).

50 The tea ceremony is a traditional Japanese way of entertaining guests, based on the adoration of the beautiful. A few friends meet in the host's tea house, typically a self-contained structure designed to give a sense of seclusion and rustic yet refined simplicity. The room is empty except for a few objects upon which attention will be focused – the tea utensils (all carefully chosen) plus a hanging scroll, a floral arrangement, and/or some other aesthetic object. The tea is enjoyed and the chosen matters discussed in a manner expressing the four qualities of harmony, respect, cleanliness and tranquility. Parallels with the secluded, serene and sparsely-furnished Farnsworth House are obvious.

51 See n.24

52 Mrs Tugendhat's encomium is quoted in Schulze, *Mies van der Rohe*, p.161–73. For an account of the ripples caused by Mies's insistence on giving clients what he thought they ought to want, rather than what they actually wanted, see Spaeth pp.68–70. For a full monograph on the building see Daniela Hammer-Tugendhat and Wolf Tegethoff, *Ludwig Mies van der Rohe: The Tugendhat House*, Vienna/New York: Springer (published after the present text was written).

53 Justus Bier's essay 'Kann Man im Haus Tugendhat wohnen?' ('Can one live in the Tugendhat House?') was published in *Die Form*, 6, 1931, pp.392 et seq, quoted in Neumeyer p.xv; Fritz and Grete Tugendhat's emphatic 'yes' is fully quoted in Tegethoff pp.97–8.

54 The story of the Resor House is told briefly in Schulze, *Mies van der Rohe*, pp.209–13 and Tegethoff pp.127–9, and in detail in Lambert, pp.160–80.

55 The desire to differentiate between the man-made building and the natural landscape has characterized much modern design. A typical quotation is from the Bauhausian architect and furniture designer Marcel Breuer (1902–81): 'A building is a man-made work, a crystallic, constructed thing. It should not imitate nature – it should be in contrast with nature.' Marcel Breuer, *Sun and Shadow*, New York: Dodd Mead, 1955, p.380.

56 Mies's designs appear to have been conceived almost at a stroke, and quickly perfected. Nothing could be further from the truth. Mies always evolved his designs via hundreds of sketches and numerous models, testing every conceivable variation of each idea in a patient search for perfection. Usually these sketches have not survived, but for the Resor project (n.54) Mies is known to have done several hundred – or perhaps over a thousand (Tegethoff p.19). He particularly liked sketching and re-sketching the spiral stair (borrowed from the Tugendhat House), and studying the detail where the cruciform columns (borrowed from the Barcelona Pavilion) met floor and ceiling.

57 Schulze, *The Farnsworth House*

58 Ibid.

59 See n.12

60 See n.14

61 See n.25

62 Neumeyer p.259

63 Ibid. pp.248–9

64 The steel skeleton with masonry infill was well-known in nineteenth-century Germany, ultimately deriving from half-timbering (Tegethoff p.101); and Mies first used this form of concealed construction in the Weissenhof Apartment Building. The Tugendhat House and Resor House are hybrids, with some steel columns hidden in walls but others standing clear as first seen in the temporary Barcelona Pavilion. In the Farnsworth House the steel frame finally reigns supreme and nothing is hidden.

65 See n.36

66 See n.12

67 Platonic doctrine holds that while we see around us many individual men, we must have an abstract conception of Man to enable us to describe so many different objects by the same name. And the same for all other sensible objects. Architects of Platonic disposition might therefore argue that behind all walls or columns or windows there is an abstract conception of Wall or Column or Window which represents that object in its ideal form – a form, presumably, of irreducible clarity and simplicity. In this spirit one may see the smooth stone rectangles of Mies's Barcelona Pavilion as representing the irreducible essence of Wall, the clean sheets of glass as representing the essence of Window, and so on. One can understand the appeal of such a quest for distilled, ideal form to Mies and his generation, who grew up with buildings and furniture whose essential forms were sometimes distorted or ornamented almost beyond recognition.

68 See n.30

69 But not miraculously so, as implied by Peter Blake when he writes that the steelwork of the Farnsworth House is so precisely welded that it 'sings like a tuning fork when it is lightly tapped' (Blake p.84). This pleasing notion, repeated by Neil Jackson (*The Modern Steel House*, London: Spon Press, 1996, p.66) and Richard Weston (*The House in the Twentieth Century*, London, Laurence King, 2002, p.155), is, alas, a romantic fiction. The welded steel structure may possibly have possessed the resonance of a tuning fork before being loaded with massive floor and roof slabs, but it certainly has not sung since.

70 *Architectural Forum*, Oct 1951, pp.156–62

71 For a discussion of the contrasting detailing techniques of the classically-inspired Mies (who strove for idealized perfection), and the arts-and-crafts-influenced Greenes (who strove for rude honesty) see Ford pp.123–60 and 261–87. While the detailing philosophies of these designers are in the above sense polar opposites, there is of course another sense in which they are akin: unlike industrial design, in which standard components are connected by standard means for speed and economy, both Mies and the Greenes expended time and money to produce one-off craftworks.

72 For the detailing of the Barcelona chair and other Miesian furniture see Spaeth pp.76–83. For the detailing of the Lange House see Ford p.269.

73 Mies's pursuit of perfect form led him on occasion to sacrifice function to aesthetics, particularly in his glass-walled pavilions. Some of his IIT campus buildings are widely known to have suffered from solar heat gain, heat loss, glare, noise penetration from outside, noise penetration within the building, roof damage, and cracking of window glass and/or ceiling plaster owing to thermal movement. A study by Skidmore Owings and Merrill in 1974 found that Crown Hall (a large clear-span pavilion completed in 1956 to house the IIT's departments of Architecture, City Planning and Design) needed a one million-dollar restoration programme, including $100,000 for a new roofing system. In 1999 Fujikawa, Johnson and Associates (see n.89) were retained to restore Crown Hall.

74 Mies's willingness to subordinate the likes and dislikes of individual clients to 'universal' values is evident from his designs and writings. The Roman and medieval buildings he most admired were described by him as 'totally impersonal' (Neumeyer p.245). Of his own work he said in the 1920s that 'questions of a general nature are of central interest. The individual becomes less and less important; his fate no longer interests us.' (ibid. p.246). His later buildings tend similarly to ignore the particularities of site, climate or orientation. In the 1960s he told Peter Carter, 'I am in fact completely opposed to the idea that a specific building should have an individual character … it should express a universal character.' (Carter p.61)

75 See n.29

76 In August 1951 the German philosopher Martin Heidegger (1889–1976) presented an important paper titled *Bauen, Wohnen, Denken* ('Building, Dwelling, Thinking') at a symposium on Man and Space in Darmstadt. Heidegger suggests that modern man no longer knows the full meaning of the act of 'dwelling', and sets out to trace the meaning of this experience to its deepest existential roots. As with Ebeling (n.29), his essay is not an easy read and remains unavailable in English; but some idea of his approach to architecture may be found in the writings of Christian Norberg-Schulz – eg *Existence, Space and Architecture* (London: Studio Vista, 1971) and *Genius Loci* (London: Academy Editions, 1980). I am indebted to Professor Dieter Holm for a translation of the essay and for the suggestion that the 'act of dwelling' (in Heidegger's sense of humankind making itself at home in the world, and at one with the world) is possibly more powerfully satisfied by the conjunction of man, architecture and nature in the Farnsworth House than by almost any other twentieth-century dwelling.

77 Schulze, *The Farnsworth House*

78 Ibid.

79 Most traditional building construction is 'layered', each layer masking imperfections in the one beneath. Thus a rough wall may be covered by a layer of plaster, which in turn is covered by a layer of paper and/or paint. Similarly, rough timber framing is covered by more accurately machined joinery, and all joints are then masked by mouldings. In addition to being visually expressive, traditional cornices, skirtings, jambs, architraves and beads therefore perform the vital function of masking rough edges, cracks and structural movement in the fabric beneath. Mies's post-1930 buildings almost completely avoid such layering. Components and joints are nakedly displayed as in a Greek temple – a design approach that is very unforgiving of imperfections.

80 For Mies's self-proclaimed commitment to rational problem-solving and industrial materials/methods see numerous statements from 1922 onwards quoted in Neumeyer pp.240–63. For his desire to develop a limited number of reproducible 'type forms' that could be adapted to many situations, thus helping to bring order to the visual chaos of twentieth-century cities, see Carter pp.37–110. On p.7 Carter quotes Mies as saying 'I have tried to make an architecture for a technological society. I have wanted to keep everything reasonable and clear – to have an architecture that anybody can do.' Mies's aversion to novel and individualistic building forms shines forth from many other statements – see for instance Neumeyer pp.324, 325, 332, 336, 338.

81 Blake pp.9, 10

82 See n.73

83 With regard to the 50 ft by 50 ft House (which could also be made 40 ft or 60 ft square to suit the client's needs), Schulze, *Mies van der Rohe*, p.261 refers to an undated clipping from the *Chicago Tribune*, held in the Mies van der Rohe Archive at the Museum of Modern Art in New York, which quotes Mies as saying: 'Since there seems to be a real need for such homes we have attempted to solve the problem by developing a steel skeleton and a core that could be used for all houses ... The interior is left open for flexibility.'

84 In an interview on the BBC Third Programme in 1959 Mies told Graeme Shankland, 'I would not like to live in a cubical house with a lot of small rooms. I would rather live on a bench in Hyde Park' (Carter p.181); and the last sentence in n.83 suggests that he believed the open plan to be viable for family houses too. But he did recognize the critical importance of size for open-plan houses. In the same interview he told Shankland that if he were designing for himself, 'I would build a simple but very large house, so that I can do inside what I like.' Similarly in 'Mies in Berlin', an interview recorded on a gramophone disc in 1966 and issued by Bauwelt Archiv, Berlin, Mies recalls telling Hugo Haring: 'Make your rooms large, Hugo, then you can use them however you like.'

85 'What Wright and his successors ... failed to realize was that the "open plan" as developed in Japan between Mies and Edith Farnsworth but refused to testify success entirely on one or both of two factors: the availability of cheap servants and/or the availability of enslaved wives ... who kept the pristine spaces in immaculate order by stashing away all the messy appurtenances that might offend the eyes of her husband or his male visitors.' For further savage comments on the impracticalities of the open plan see pp.31–6 of Peter Blake's *Form Follows Fiasco: Why modern architecture hasn't worked*, Boston/Toronto, Little Brown and Company, 1977.

86 Karl Freund, a craftsman who worked on the Farnsworth House, was subpoenaed to give evidence in the court case between Mies and Edith Farnsworth but refused to testify against either. He later said, 'They are equally guilty of making a thing without a solid contract ... She didn't understand the house. Mies should have made much clearer to her what she was getting. It is a beautiful museum piece, but she didn't like to live in it.' David Spaeth, 'The Farnsworth House Revisited', *Fine Homebuilding*, Apr/May 1988, p.37. Quoted on p.67 of *The Modern Steel House* (n.69 above).

87 For the Tallon House, Villa Maesen and Skywood House see pp.23–9 of *The House in the Twentieth Century* (n.69 above).

88 During the 1970s Dr Edith Farnsworth retired from practice and moved to a villa near Florence in Italy. She died in 1977 aged 74.

89 Dirk Lohan is the son of Professor Wolfgang Lohan and Mies van der Rohe's daughter Marianne. He joined Mies's practice in 1962, soon after graduation, and became his grandfather's most trusted assistant. After Mies's death the practice passed to his associates Conterato, Fujikawa and Lohan. This firm was commissioned to carry out the restoration of the Farnsworth House in 1972, with Dirk Lohan personally in charge. After the 1996 flood Dirk Lohan, now in practice as Lohan Associates, was again commissioned to undertake the necessary repairs.

90 This account is taken largely from Schulze, *The Farnsworth House*, with additional detail supplied by Lord Palumbo in letters to the present author.

91 Flat roofs are risk-prone in cold-winter climates if the building is heated and insulated, and if the roof insulation is located *beneath* the waterproof membrane (as was standard practice until recently). In winter moisture-laden warm air may rise through the ceiling, filter through the insulation layer and be trapped against the cold underside of the waterproof membrane. The latter will chill the moisture-laden air, possibly to below dew-point temperature, in which case the air/vapour mixture trapped beneath will condense into droplets of water. These may then soak into the insulation layer, reducing its insulating properties, encouraging mould growth and staining the ceiling below. Fixing a vapour-proof barrier beneath the insulation (as was done in the Farnsworth House in 1972) will avoid the problem, but only if this barrier remains totally vapour-proof which is difficult to guarantee. The best solution is to place all insulation *above* the waterproof membrane (the so-called 'inverted roof') and not below it.

92 Schulze, *The Farnsworth House*

93 The new approach route to Farnsworth House happily recalls a strategy of 'gradual revelation' Mies van der Rohe used at both the Barcelona Pavilion and Tugendhat House. In both cases the interior is reached only after visitors have walked the length of the building, then made a right-angle turn on to a raised terrace, followed by another right-angled turn into the building – see figures 49 and 50. In later life the increasingly stern Mies abandoned such theatrical effects for extreme directness. The approach routes to both his Seagram Building (1957–9) and New National Gallery (1962–8) are frontal and arrow-straight.

94 See n.89

SELECT BIBLIOGRAPHY

This short list is not comprehensive but identifies a number of core references. Extensive bibliographies will be found in Schulze, Spaeth and Tegethoff below.

Blake, Peter, *Mies van der Rohe*, London: Penguin Books, 1963

Carter, Peter, *Mies van der Rohe at Work*, London: Phaidon Press, 1999

De Sola-Morales, Cirici, and Ramos, *Mies van der Rohe – the Barcelona Pavilion*, Barcelona: Gustavo Gili, 1993

Ford, Edward R, *The Details of Modern Architecture*, Cambridge, MA/London: MIT Press, 1990. See especially ch.9, 'Ludwig Mies van der Rohe and the Steel Frame', pp.261–87

Johnson, Philip, *Mies van der Rohe*, 3rd edition, London: Secker & Warburg, 1978

Jordy, William H, *American Buildings and their Architects*, vol.4, New York: Anchor Books, 1976. See especially ch.IV, 'The Laconic Splendour of the Metal Frame: Ludwig Mies van der Rohe's 860 Lake Shore Apartments and his Seagram Building', pp.221–77

Lambert, Phyllis, *Mies in America*, New York: Harry N Abrams, 2001

Lohan, Dirk, *Farnsworth House, Plano, Illinois, 1945–50*, Global Architecture Detail, Tokyo: ADA Edita, 1976

Neumeyer, Fritz, *The Artless Word*, Cambridge, MA/London: MIT Press, 1991

Schulze, Franz, *Mies van der Rohe: A Critical Biography*, Chicago/London: University of Chicago Press, 1985

Schulze, Franz, *The Farnsworth House*, 1997. A 32-page illustrated booklet available to visitors to the Farnsworth House

Spaeth, David, *Mies van der Rohe*, London: The Architectural Press, 1985

Tegethoff, Wolf, *Mies van der Rohe: The Villas and Country Houses*, Cambridge, MA/London: MIT Press, 1985

DIMENSIONS

	Imperial	Metric
Overall length	77 ft 3 in	23.546 m
Internal width	28 ft 8 in	8.738 m
Internal height	9 ft 6 in	2.896 m
Internal floor area	2,215 sq ft	205.83 sq m
Deck length	55 ft	16.764 m
Deck width	22 ft	6.706 m
Deck area	1,210 sq ft	112.42 sq m
Floor level above ground	± 5 ft	± 1.5 m
Deck level above ground	± 2 ft	± 0.6 m
Stanchion spacing along length of house	22 ft	6.706 m
Floor & roof cantilevers beyond end stanchions	5 ft 7 in	1.702 m
Floor module		
Length	2 ft 9 in	838 mm
Width	2 ft	610 mm
Entrance door offset	1 ft	305 mm
Core unit length	24 ft 6 in	7.468 m
Core unit width	12 ft	3.658 m
Core unit height	7 ft 6 in	2.286 m
Storage cabinet length	12 ft	3.658 m
Storage cabinet depth	2 ft 2 in	0.660 m
Storage cabinet height	6 ft	1.829 m
Kitchen area width	4 f	1.20 m
Sitting area width	12 ft	3.70 m
Dining area width	17 ft	5.20 m
Sleeping area width	12 ft	3.70 m
Steelwork		
Fascia height	15 in	381 mm
Stanchion size	8 in square	203 mm square

MATERIALS
(before renovation)

Structure Wide-flange rolled steel joists
Wall framing Flat steel bars welded together
Wall glazing 1/4 in (6.4mm) polished plate glass
Door framing Kawneer narrow stile aluminium
Door glazing 1/4 in (6.4mm) polished plate glass
Floor and deck 1 1/4 in (31.8mm) thick travertine slabs laid with ± 1/16 in (1.6mm) joints
Roof finish Gravel bedded in pitch on 6 layers of roof felting on 2in (51 mm) foam glass slabs bedded in asphalt on 1 ply vapour seal membrane with two moppings of pitch
Ceiling Plaster on metal lath
Core unit Primavera-faced plywood panels on timber framing
Storage cabinet Teak-faced plywood panels on timber framing

FARNSWORTH HOUSE CHRONOLOGY

1945
Mies van der Rohe meets Dr Edith Farnsworth

1945
Dr Farnsworth commissions Mies to design a weekend retreat at the Fox River, near Plano, 60 miles west of Chicago

1946
The basic design of the Farnsworth House is fixed

1949
Dr Farnsworth receives an inheritance which enables construction to begin

1951
The house is completed

1951
Mies sues Dr Farnsworth for unpaid fees. Dr Farnsworth countersues, alleging a cost over-run and design faults

1953
The lawsuit is settled in Mies's favour

1953
An article titled 'The Threat to the Next America', an attack on the Farnsworth House and on Mies van der Rohe, is published in the American magazine *House Beautiful*

1954
The Fox River rises 1.2 m above internal floor level, damaging finishes and furnishings

1967
Kendall County compulsorily purchases part of Dr Farnsworth's property, widens and raises the road along the western boundary of the site, and moves the road closer to the house

1968
Dr Farnsworth advertises the house for sale

1968
Mies van der Rohe dies

1971
Dr Farnsworth sells the house to Mr Peter (later Lord) Palumbo

1972
Mr Palumbo employs Mr Dirk Lohan to renovate the house

1977
Dr Farnsworth dies at the age of 74 in Italy, where she has lived for some years

1996
The Fox River rises 1.5 m above internal floor level, breaking the glass walls and causing severe internal damage. Lord Palumbo employs Dirk Lohan to renovate the house

1997
The Fox river rises 0.3 m above internal floor level, causing minor damage

1997
Lord Palumbo opens the restored house to the public

KEY DATES IN THE LIFE OF MIES VAN DER ROHE

3 March 1886
Born in Aachen, Germany

1904
Moves to Berlin

1905–7
Holds series of positions in private architectural practice in Berlin

1908–11
Works in Berlin studio of Peter Behrens

1911–14
In private architectural practice in Berlin

1914–18
Military service

1919–37
In private architectural practice in Berlin

1921
Co-founder of G (Gestaltung magazine) in Berlin

1921–5
Director of Architectural Exhibits, November Group, Berlin

1925
Founder, Zehner Ring, Berlin

1926–32
First Vice-President, Deutscher Werkbund, Berlin

1927
Director of the Weissenhofsiedlung, Stuttgart

1930–2
Director of the Bauhaus at Dessau

1931
Director of the Werkbund section 'The Dwelling' at the Berlin Building Exhibition

1932–3
Director of the Bauhaus in Berlin

1933
The Bauhaus closes

1937–8
Emigrates to the USA

1938–59
Director of Architecture at the Armour Institute of Technology in Chicago (later to become the Illinois Institute of Technology)

1938–69
In private architectural practice in Chicago

1946–51
Designs and oversees construction of the Farnsworth House

17 August 1969
Dies in Chicago

SELECT CHRONOLOGY OF WORKS

Houses by Mies van der Rohe

This list excludes Mies's multistorey apartment blocks, except for the seminal apartment block designs of 1926–7. However, it includes the Barcelona Pavilion which is not a house but was so house-like, and its influence on Mies's later houses so seminal, that it could not be omitted. A complete schedule of all Mies's buildings and projects is given in both Lambert and Schulze (see Select Bibliography).

1907
Riehl House, Berlin-Neubabelsberg

1910–11
Perls House (later the Fuchs House), Berlin-Zehlendorf

1912
Project: Kroller-Muller House, Wassenaar, Netherlands

1912–13
Werner House, Berlin-Zehlendorf

1913
House on the Heerstrasse, Berlin

1914
Project: House for the Architect, Berlin-Werder

1914–17
Urbig House, Berlin-Neubabelsberg

1921
Project: Petermann House, Berlin-Neubabelsberg

1921–2
Kempner House, Berlin-Charlottenburg

1921–2
Feldman House, Berlin-Grünewald

1922
Eichstaedt House, Berlin-Wannsee

1923
Project: Concrete Country House

1923
Project: Lessing House, Berlin-Neubabelsberg

1923
Project: Ryder House, Wiesbaden

1923
Project: Kiepenheuer House

1923–4
Project: Brick Country House

1924–6
Mosler House, Berlin-Neubabelsberg

1925
Project: Dexel House, Jena

1925
Project: Eliat House, Nedlitz

1925–7
Wolf House, Guben

1925–7
Weissenhof Housing Colony and Exhibition

1926–7
Municipal Housing Development on the Afrikanischestrasse, Berlin

1927
Apartment Building for Weissenhoff Housing Colony, Stuttgart

1927
Glass Room for Exhibition, Stuttgart

1927–30
Esters House, Krefeld

1927–30
Lange House, Krefeld

1928
Addition to Fuchs House (formerly Perls House), Berlin-Zehlendor

1928–9
German Pavilion at the Barcelona Exposition

1928–30
Tugendhat House, Brno

1929
Project: Nolde House, Berlin-Zehlendorf

1930
Addition to Henke House, Essen

1931
Model house and apartment for Berlin Building Exposition

1931–8
Projects: series of Court Houses

1932
Project: Gericke House, Berlin-Wannsee

1932–3
Lemke House, Berlin-Hohenschonhausen

1933
Severain House, Wiesbaden

1934
Project: Mountain House for the Architect

1934
Project: Glass House on a Hillside

1934
Project: House on a Terrace

1935
Project: Hubbe House, Magdeburg

1935
Project: Ulrich Lange House, Krefeld

1937–8
Project: Resor House, Wyoming

1946–7
Project: Cantor House, Indianapolis

1946–51
Farnsworth House, Illinois

1950
Project: Caine House, Winnetka, Illinois

1950–1
Project: Steel Frame Prefabricated Row House

1950–1
Project: 50 by 50 House

1951–2
McCormick House, Elmhurst

1951–3
Morris Greenwald House, Westport

Clear-span Pavilions by Mies van der Rohe

1928–9
German Pavilion, Barcelona

1942
Project: Concert Hall

1945–6
Project: Cantor Drive-in Restaurant, Indianapolis

1946–51
Farnsworth House, Illinois

1947
Project: Theatre for IIT

1947
Project: IIT Gym and Swimming Pool

1949–52
IIT Chapel

1950–6
IIT Crown Hall

1950–1
Project: 50 by 50 House

1952–3
Project: National Theatre, Mannheim

1953–4
Project: Convention Hall, Chicago

1954
Museum of Fine Arts, Houston

1954–8
Cullinan Hall, Houston

1957
Project: Bacardi Office Building, Santiago

1960–1
Project: Schaefer Museum, Schweinfurt

1962–7
New National Gallery, Berlin

1963–9
Dominion Centre, Toronto

1966–9
Project: Museum Addition, Houston